1983

YEARS OF HIGH PURPOSE

FROM TRUSTEESHIP TO NATIONHOOD

YEARS OF HIGH PURPOSE

from Trusteeship to Nationhood

by Mason Sears

Library of Congress Catalog Card Number: 80-5161

YEARS OF HIGH PURPO

from Trusteeship to Nationho

by Mason Sear

with a preface by Henry Cabot Lo
and an introduction by Julius Nye

UNIVERSITY PRESS OF AMERICA, WASHINGT

The record which follows is a story of frustration, my personal frustration, in failing to persuade the U.S. State Department not to reverse traditional U.S. Policy toward self-determination, meaning national freedom, for all peoples —Africans in particular.

Contents

Africa in 1979

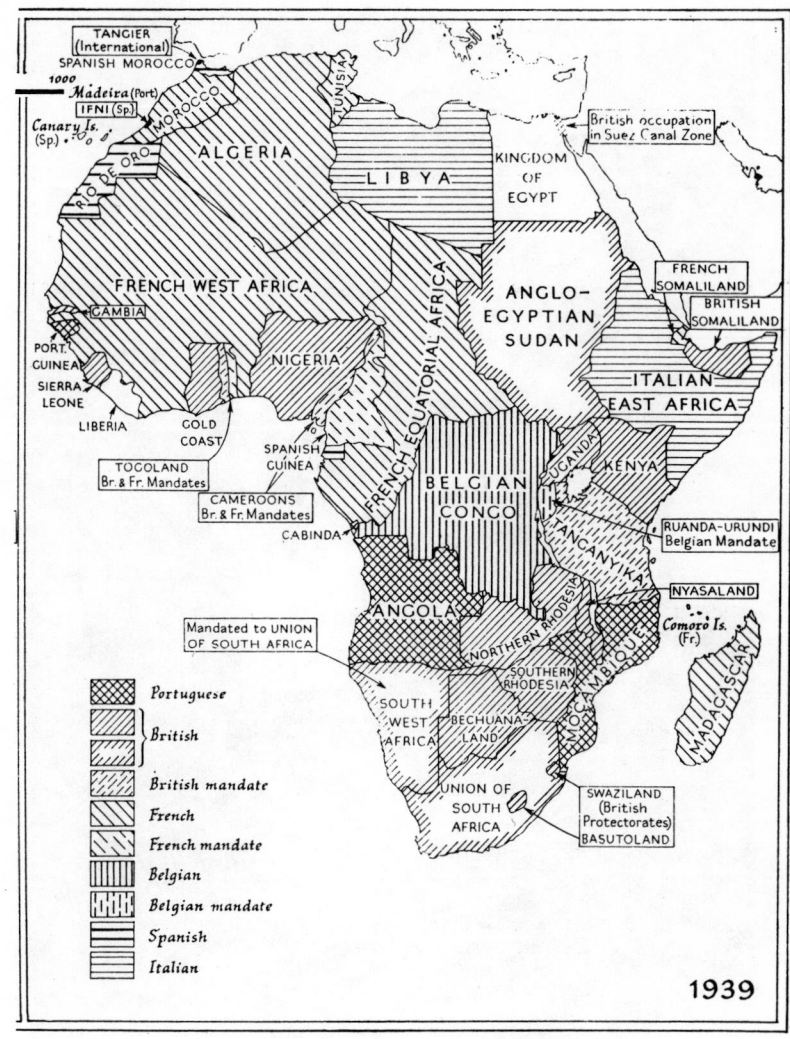

The Colonial Empires 1939

Swearing in of Ambassador Mason Sears by U.S. Representative to the United Nations, Henry Cabot Lodge.

Preface

Henry Cabot Lodge

In the late 1950's a process began which changed the face of Africa, shifted international relationships all over the world and altered forever the future of the United Nations. This event was the conversion of areas which had long been European colonies into independent nation-states. The work of ushering the new states into the family of nations was done by the Trusteeship Council of the United Nations.

For those whose knowledge of the United Nations is a little rusty, it could be said that the United Nations contains three councils: the Security Council (which deals with threats to the peace), the Economic and Social Council and the Trusteeship Council. This last included representatives of colonial powers, to wit: Great Britain, France, Italy, Australia, New Zealand and the United States (because we are trustees for the tiny Pacific Islands) and an equivalent number of representatives of states which had no colonies. The representative of the United States in the Trusteeship Council was Ambassador Mason Sears.

For Sears the year 1960 was a great climax. For years he had travelled throughout Africa, visiting these one-time colonies. It was his duty to make up his mind whether each one was ready for self-government. As Representative of the United States to the United Nations at this time I soon learned that in doing his work he had become famous and admired in the African world. His statements were front page news in their press. Pictures of him standing or moving against some tropical background were frequently published there. Wherever he went, he made friends for the United States.

However, he was also working in a field of bitter controversy. Those who hated to see colonialism go—quite naturally—attacked him in Washington. Vigorous debates ensued. The then Secretary of State, Mr. Dulles, had doubts, as a reading of these pages will reveal and his disagreements with Sears are fully set forth in the ensuing pages. But Secretary of State Christian Herter had the last word. In a letter to Sears on the occasion of Sears' retirement from government service, he said:

> "You can look back with satisfaction on a difficult job well done. You have represented the United States faithfully and ably in the Trusteeship Council. Your close friendships with a number of important African leaders have created a large reservoir of good will for Americans in general in this key area of the world. Moreover, I am fully aware of how much your efforts in the Council, with the press and before private groups, have contributed to American awareness of the problem and challenges of this rapidly-evolving continent."

I remember the day when Sears came to me to say that all the areas were exercising self-government and that the work of the Trusteeship Council was ended. To his great satisfaction, his activities had helped to work him out of a job.

This book contains the record of these angry and exciting days of Sears' work on African matters—in Africa, in Washington and at the United Nations. It is unique. None of the controversies are concealed or glossed over. No one in the U.S. government had his knowledge of these questions—or could possibly have had it. This report, just completed before Sears' death, is an indispensable part of the history of our times, and of aspects of that history which are full of fast moving and complicated implications for the future. His was a superb accomplishment. Whoever would understand the sub-surface factors underlying our relations with the new African states, with all they mean for the United States, should read this book.

Sears' official position in the U.S. and in the U.S. government opened doors for him when he went to Africa. There were few indeed who had his contacts. He was thus in touch with leading Africans.

These contacts, added to his own sensitive political instincts, enabled him to sense how these new nation-states would evolve. Later and more recent events amply justified Sears' estimate that a wave of independence and self-government was pouring over Africa which could not be stopped. Such indeed has been the case.

Henry Cabot Lodge
July 25, 1979

Introduction

Julius K. Nyerere

Mr. Mason Sears, the author of this book, was once regarded by the colonial authorities of Britain—and probably also of France and Belgium—as a dangerous and irresponsible American, dabbling in matters which he did not understand, and doing considerable damage in the process. His own Secretary of State, Mr. Dulles, seems to have had a similar view. Leaders of African nationalist movements, on the other hand, regarded him as an understanding and anti-colonialist American official—and perhaps misunderstood the limitations on his freedom of action and official speech.

It was in those days—while a "political agitator"—that I first met Mr. Sears. He was the American representative on the Trusteeship Council of the United Nations, and a member of the 'Visiting Mission' to Tanganyika in 1954. He was thus a man whom the Administering Power of the Tanganyika Trust Territory had to deal with.

There is little doubt but that for many of the British Government officials in Tanganyika, the task was a somewhat disconcerting one. Mr. Sears was a good guest in that he enjoyed travelling around the country, and was appreciative of the developments he was shown. On the other hand he had this somewhat unorthodox habit—it was unorthodox in Tanganyika then!—of being friendly to, and interested in the ideas and attitudes of, the indigenous inhabitants. He even took seriously the political pretensions of the nascent Tanganyika African National Union (formed only a few months previously) and its leader—who was then a young Secondary School teacher earning a few hundred shillings a month!

Twelve years after Tanganyika's independence it is not easy to remember, and still less easy to appreciate, the great furor which was caused by the 1954 Visiting Mission's Report that a time table should be set for Tanganyika's (and Ruanda/Urundi's) independence, and that these Trust Territories should become sovereign states within 20-25 years. Nationalism, and the right to at least 'flag-independence,' is now accepted by virtually all members of the United Nations—at least in their public pronouncements. Yet this recent history is not irrelevant to current political attitudes between the new and old states; nor is the background to United States policies on that issue without interest for contemporary politics.

Mr. Sears was very much a loyal American public servant concerned with the future of his country and its reputation in the world. Unfortunately for him, he was also an American who believed in the ideals of his country as exemplified in the Declaration of American Independence and the great words in which that Declaration was expressed. It therefore seemed to him that his country's membership of the Trusteeship Council as an "administering power" was a temporary quirk of post-war political history and that America really belonged with the forces of national freedom. Consequently, when instructions came from the State Department that he should speak in the Trusteeship Council on the side of "caution," he obeyed the letter but not the spirit of his instructions. Further, when a member of the Trusteeship Council Visiting Mission to East Africa, he felt that he was there as an American to make serious investigations about how progress could best be made towards independence for the Trusteeship Territories of Ruanda/Urundi, Tanganyika and Somalia.

The nationalist leaders who met Mr. Sears at the time

of that Mission were, it now appears, as naive as he in relation to America's policies during the cold war of the 1950's. We had read about the American War of Independence, and had heard of President Roosevelt's statements that America was not fighting in the Second World War in order to perpetuate European empires but in order to support the freedom struggle everywhere. To us, therefore, Mr. Sears was both an understanding man, and a good representative of his country. We were perhaps less surprised than he at the reaction of the British Government to the Visiting Mission's recommendations on Tanganyika; but our surprise was probably greater—because our ignorance was then greater—about the reaction of his own Secretary of State.

Even if our surprise was greater, it is probable that our chagrin was less. For it was Mr. Sears who was required to stand up in the Trusteeship Council and, on behalf of his Government, repudiate the stand taken by the Mission of which he was a leading member! A letter from Mr. Dulles to Ambassador Lodge giving these instructions is printed almost in full in the most revealing pages of this book.

That letter is important because it illustrates a practical example of power politics at work. The merits of the matter under discussion were regarded as irrelevant; what mattered to Mr. Dulles was the possible reaction of America's Allies to a particular stand on colonial questions and what effect it might have on other American interests elsewhere in the world—with particular reference to the territories America "administered".

This cynical attitude towards political justice on the part of the big powers is now a commonplace of international politics, but it is one which we small and weak countries of Africa adopt, and fail to adopt, at our peril. On the one hand we have no military strength, and have in the past built very little economic strength. Therefore it is only on the basis of political morality that we can "justify" and maintain our national sovereignty, or extend the freedom of our continent. We, the weak nations, have therefore a national duty, as well as an international opportunity, to stand by the basic principles of human equality and justice in all our domestic and international policies. These principles are the basis for our existence and also our most basic strength internationally and externally.

Yet on the other hand this Dulles' letter illustrates, and the events of the 1960's and the early 1970's in relation to Southern Africa demonstrate, that the big powers of the world do not think in these terms of principle at all. They respond to power, and apparently—at least within any reasonable period of time—to nothing else. We cannot afford to neglect that reality any more than we can afford to abandon our own commitment to political principles.

The importance of this lesson in reality is now being recognized by the Third World. So much so, that there has been a change in what we regard as relevant questions in relation to international affairs. We now know that there are slim chances that the rich nations of the world will respond to an appeal to their political principles. We shall not stop trying to avoid violence and suffering by making such appeals, but we no longer rely upon a positive response as a solution to the problems of colonialism and exploitation. Instead, we give priority to two other questions. The first, is when and how we poor nations will succeed in marshalling and using our collective economic power—for the Third World does have strength in unity despite the separate weakness of our states. The second question, which is of great importance to the world, is whether we shall ourselves always use that power for the ends of justice and human equality; whether, in other words, power and principle will for once be on the same side.

The first question has already begun to be answered in practice. The oil countries have flexed their muscles in such a way that never again will they be able to be disregarded. Other countries producing specialised minerals of importance to the world's industrialized and wealthy countries are now in the process of organising themselves for a united stand. These associations of specialised producers may be compared with the 19th century British craft unions of skilled workers. The unity of all the poor countries, like the unions of industrial or unskilled workers, will come later. But it will certainly come, and the power situation in the world will then be very different from what it has been in the recent years. The "Trade Union of the Third World" will not be easy to create, but once established, it will be able to bring radical change to the existing international relationships.

How such Trade Union power will in fact be used is another question. In one respect it cannot fail—at least at the beginning—to favour the cause of justice and equality. For this economic weapon will for the first time be wielded by the poor countries against the rich; at the minimum it will therefore bring a little redistribution of world resources in favor of the deprived nations. It could be, of course, that in the economic sphere the newly powerful nations will simply replace the old exploiters of the remaining poor—that in international terms the "nouveau riche" will be economic oppressors of the poor nations quite as bad as their predecessors. That possibility exists. Equally likely, however, is the possibility that the existing oppressors of the poor will try to use the threat of "nouveau riche" nations as a way of perpetuating their own actual and continuing exploitation of all the Third World! In other words they will try to continue their economic domination by further policies of "divide and rule".

Such an attempt will probably have some short term successes; but in the long run it cannot alter the march of history, any more than it can hide the political transformation which will come from a comparative weakening of the existing colonial powers—for the oil states do not have colonies and the existing wealthy nations do! And in any case one essential fact remains: the rich nations of the world believe in power, and respond to power, so sooner or later the poor countries will learn to create and use the only power they could possess—unity.

It was this kind of confrontation politics between the New World and the Third World which Mr. Sears was working in the fifties to avoid, although he was thinking only in political terms. Yet even in those terms, successive governments in the world have failed to understand what he was saying. Many still do not appear to understand—or at least they do not act on such an understanding. For Mr. Sears was arguing in the 1950's that a people cannot indefinitely be governed without their consent and that any endeavor to perpetuate colonial or racist rule would result in violence. That simple and very basic truth has been proved time and again throughout history—injustice cannot be sustained indefinitely, and if peaceful protests do not succeed in bringing change, then the violence of oppression will be met by the violence of liberation. Unfortunately, few governing elites seem able or willing to recognise and to apply this simple truth to their own position. Tanganyika was lucky in that a combination of circumstances did lead to such recognition. Despite the hysterical reaction of the British Government in 1955 to proposals that the country should become independent within 20 years, Uhuru was in fact celebrated at the end of 1961 (6 years) and the people of my country were spared the horrors of violence.

There are other reflections provoked by the events referred to in this book. In particular there is the question of what an individual should do when there is a serious clash between his own beliefs and the policies of the government or organisation he serves, or even between his beliefs and the laws of the society in which he lives.

This is an inescapable problem for individuals in the modern world. For years after the last world war there was discussion about the responsibility of ordinary German civilians for the crimes committed by the Nazi regime in Germany and other parts of Europe. But the issue is still a live one, today. What is the answer for individual South Africans who reject the principles of apartheid, whether they are black or white? They cannot all leave their country—where would they go? Do we then demand they stand up and shout, and thus face death or incarceration in Robin Island or in the prison farms? How many of those who answer that question in the affirmative from the safety of other parts of Africa or of Europe can honestly state that they would do so themselves? But it is said that at least people should refuse to carry out orders they know to be wrong; they should resign from their official positions; they should boycott the administration. Leaving aside the fact that the alternative to employment may be starvation, we have still in honesty to ask ourselves whether it is in fact always unjustified and untrue for a man to argue that by staying in his post he may be able to help some individuals, alleviate some suffering, and delay if not altogether deflect some injustices against others. There may be times when an individual feels he can fulfill his duty of opposition and still serve within the system. Obviously such reasoning can be an excuse for conformity, and alliance, with evil; it can indicate a cowardly unwillingness to make personal sacrifice for truth. But also it can sometimes reflect a man's honest attempt to solve the insoluble problem he is faced with. And this is quite apart from the question of the appropriate strategy and tactics for opposition to evil in different times and circumstances.

Most of us are fortunate in that this question of individual responsibility in the face of evil or mistaken policies is not put before us in such horrific terms as it faced the people of Nazi Germany or as it faces honest people in South Africa today. But the basic question of individual responsibility for the actions of his collective group still remains. None of us can hope to do anything useful for our society or for the world in isolation. We have to be members of an administration, or a political party, or a religious group—or something. And whatever group we join we shall never agree with everything which it does or says or stands for. For the sake of the strength that comes through unity we have to make compromises with the totality of our beliefs. The question, therefore, becomes not whether we shall support things we disagree with but where shall we draw the line? At what point do we sacrifice unity for principle, rather than beliefs for united action on other beliefs? When you have an important disagreement with the institution of which you are a part, should you argue that by working within the system you can influence it or perhaps change it; or should you always resign under such circumstances?

There are people who feel that they know the answers to such questions as these for all places, all times and all circumstances. There are others who are never prepared to make a judgement of anyone, but argue that the whole truth about a man's work, influence and attitude can be known only to himself and that no one not faced with his problem has the right to criticise his decision. In practice the first attitude seems remarkably unintelligent as well as being unconstructive; the second reaction is a further endeavour to escape the responsibilities of life. But the problem is a real one which few people can altogether avoid as they go through life.

Mr. Sears' book does not debate these serious philosophical questions. It is an account of his own experiences, and it is a very personal account in the sense that he details what he saw and how he reacted to things he was shown. The book is revealing of the man, and within the limits of his time and place he was helpful to the freedom movements of East Africa during an important period. Few of us can claim more. We play our role as our conscience demands and to the best of our ability.

Chapter I

Beginnings and Stirrings

> The record which follows is a story of frustration, my
> personal frustration, in failing to persuade the U.S. State
> Department not to reverse traditional U.S. policy toward
> self-determination, meaning national freedom, for all
> peoples—Africans in particular.

It was a moment before midnight on the eve of
Independence Day, Dec. 9, 1961, in Dar es Salaam. The huge crowd
in the floodlit stadium was silent. Drawn up in the foreground was a
battalion of the King's African Rifles while in the center was a
flagstaff. On one side of it stood the British Governor of Tanganyika,
on the other side the figure of Julius Nyerere, father of his country
and now the first Prime Minister of Tanganyika. At the stroke of
midnight the band struck up "God Save the Queen" while the British
Union Jack was slowly lowered. In its place, the flag of the new
nation of Tanganyika was raised while the band played the national
anthem. The moment of independence had come. The crowd roared
its approval.

All over Africa similar scenes were enacted as dozens
of former colonies and protectorates became independent. The
European-dominated colonial system was at an end and in an

1

unprecedented decolonization process. Between 1956 and 1968 no less than 30 African states gained their freedom from foreign control.

The account which follows describes some of the important events which occurred during these last years of colonialism in Africa. It also traces the official U.S. response to the development of African nationalism, a response which was a disappointment to many Americans as well as millions of Africans and Asians.

Appointed by President Eisenhower as U.S. Representative to the United Nations under his chief Representative, Henry Cabot Lodge, I was given a front row seat at the U.N. for many of the events of this period; it was my duty to represent the United States on the Trusteeship Council, that important body which was to supervise the administration of the International Trust Territories and oversee their eventual independence.

During World War II as the Allies defeated Germany, Italy and Japan, diplomatic efforts were undertaken to create the United Nations. United States policy toward the colonies and other dependent areas of both our allies and our enemies was ambiguous. Some American officials felt that total independence for these trusteeship areas was the only solution, while others—such as John Foster Dulles and Harold Stassen—felt that it was more important to placate our European allies and accept the retention of colonial status. However, by January, 1945, there was general agreement that the broad objectives of U.S. policy should be the promotion of the advancement of dependent peoples through international collaboration and the encouragement and assistance to these peoples in governing and sustaining themselves.

Yet, despite these directives, and in the face of President Roosevelt's policy, there was some feeling that there should be no discussion of Trusteeship at San Francisco. However, Mr. Ben Gerig, my future Assistant at the U.N., pointed out that there was great risk in not discussing Trusteeship as it had been decided upon at the Yalta Conference. This view was firmly supported by Secretary of State Stettinius, the head of the San

Francisco delegation, who stated that President Roosevelt thought Trusteeship should be discussed at San Francisco.

In the end, however, events were to overtake the delegation. The force for an American policy favoring independence came from FDR and when he died, men like Stettinius and Gerig continued to fight what was a rear-guard action for an independence policy. But the tide was against them, and, in the end, the delegation decided to maintain a pro-self-government position under the assumption that it implied that independence was the goal for all people capable of it.

Prior to his death, while the U.N. Charter was being drafted, President Roosevelt clearly stated his opposition to colonialism: "To deny the objective of independence would sow the seeds of the next World War . . . We should undertake leadership and indicate to [colonial] peoples that we do not back the imperial role of a handful of nations."

President Roosevelt also felt that the issue had serious implications for future relations between the U.S. and the developing world:

> Independence as a goal for all peoples who aspire to it . . . has been the traditional and sacred policy of [the U.S.]. It has been exemplified in our policy in the Philippines. . . . An excellent opportunity is afforded to make a profitable gesture on behalf of the peoples of . . . [the colonial world].

A similar point of view was taken by Ambassador Joseph C. Grew, the Acting Secretary of State during the San Francisco Conference. In a letter to Secretary of State Stettinius, chairman of the U.S. delegation at San Francisco, Ambassador Grew wrote that Russia, not the United States, might emerge as the champion of the developing nations:

3

> At his press conference Molotov is reported to have stated that Russia will take the initiative in having the International Organization clothed with power actively to promote self-government for dependent peoples. Although this has been OUR historic role, Russia, I fear, may appear before the world as the champion of all dependent peoples. Molotov's move may confirm in the minds of the people of Asia their already strong suspicion that the Anglo-American powers are not their real champions and will turn to Russia as their more outspoken friend and spokesman.

As was shown by the public opinion polls of that time, President Roosevelt's position was quite in accord with the anti-colonial leanings of most Americans. These polls also showed that most Americans were in favor of firm U.S. support for the U.N. In response to public opinion, President Truman, in 1945, decided to raise the status of U.S. Representative to the U.N. to cabinet rank.

President Eisenhower, like President Truman, was committed to the success of the U.N. and, therefore, maintained the U.S. Ambassador to the U.N. as a member of his cabinet. However, he did appoint John Foster Dulles, a man quite critical of the U.N., as his Secretary of State. In spite of this seeming inconsistency, Eisenhower did not let Dulles' ideas deter him in his desire to strengthen the U.N. This commitment to international cooperation is best indicated by the remarkable speech the President made before the General Assembly in 1960. In this speech, which was very well received, he stated that:

> The drive of self-determination and of rising human aspirations is creating a new world of independent nations in Africa. The first proposition I place before you is that only through the U.N. organization, can humanity make real and universal progress toward a goal of peace with justice. I believe that to support the U.N. organization and its properly constituted mechanisms

and selected officers is the road of greatest promise and peaceful progress. To attempt to hinder or stultify the U.N., or to deprecate its importance, is to contribute to world unrest and indeed to incite the crises that from time to time so disturb all men. The U.S. stands squarely and unequivocably in support of the U.N. and those acting under its mandate in the interest of peace.

This strong pro-U.N. position taken by President Eisenhower created a serious conflict with the Department of State and its head, John Foster Dulles, a conflict graphically described by Ambassador Robert Murphy in his book, *Diplomat Among Warriors:*

> Personally I never regarded the U.N. as a divine machine from which happy solutions to our problems would miraculously flow. Nor have I feared the consequences, even if the U.N. should collapse utterly. The other day a friend exclaimed: "That would be the end of everything!" But it just wouldn't be the end of everything. I always have tried to take a practical view of the U.N. organization as an apparatus which is, or can be, useful to the U.S. in its diplomacy. This also was the policy of Secretary Dulles . . . Dulles respected the U.N. but he also regarded it at times as a receptacle where almost any thorny problem could be unloaded and stored away and eventually forgotten.

However, President Eisenhower did not view the U.N. as an organization without any real political standing or clout and his appointment of Henry Cabot Lodge as Representative to the United Nations underscored the importance with which he treated the organization.

Lodge's position with respect to the U.N. can best be expressed in his own words:

> The world is already a better place than it would have
> been were there no U.N. . . . The earth's peoples are
> interdependent. The members of the U.N. must,
> therefore, develop the will to bring about a rapid
> expansion of its effectiveness. It is up to the members.
> They cannot duck the responsibility for there really is no
> alternative.

Throughout this entire period, Ambassador Lodge showed me great consideration by deliberately giving me a free hand in my efforts to emphasize the importance of nationalism and its bearing upon the emergence of African nations into independence.

Although the tradition of U.S. policy was to support independence, and despite Dulles' hesitancy in this regard, I was given no instructions on assuming my post at the U.N. All I had was the U.N. Charter and my knowledge of traditional U.S. policy and American public opinion to guide me.

From the beginning of my tenure at the U.N., it was apparent that although the cold war between Russia and the West remained the basic and most dangerous issue confronting the U.N., it was the anti-colonial issue that aroused the greatest emotional response among the delegates. On one side was the growing influence of the Afro-Asian bloc of nations led by India and strongly backed by the Soviet Union. On the other side, fighting a rear-guard action, stood the representatives of the colonial empires, supported by the U.S. This support was given not so much out of any colonial sympathy but because Secretary Dulles' inordinate concern that any break in our unity with our NATO allies would undermine European defenses against Russian expansionism. To be on the imperial side of the colonial issue was particularly uncomfortable for the U.S., not only in view of its long anti-colonial history, but also because of the U.N.'s professed goal of promoting self-government and decolonization.

The impetus which the U.N. gave to African self-government can hardly be exaggerated. It brought together anti-colonial spokesmen from all over the world, for the U.N. not only included official representatives of many member nations, but also unofficial petitioners appearing for nationalist organizations based in every part of Africa. It provided a world-wide forum from which the case against colonialism could be vigorously championed and clearly accelerated their progress toward independence.

What made this forum so effective was the widespread nature of the U.N. publicity machinery. The U.N. Journal printed summaries of each day's meetings in English and French. The Department of Public Information, with its outlets all over the world, published books, pamphlets and magazines describing the work of the U.N. Documentary films were shown in over 90 countries, with sound tracks in more than two dozen languages. Radio news broadcasts by the U.N. staff went out in 34 languages. With such facilities at hand, it was no wonder that the U.N. had become a political mecca which had attracted every African leader who could afford the long journey to New York.

Had there been no U.N., a policy of "divide and conquer" might have continued to impede all African nationalist movements for they would have remained generally isolated from one another. Lacking U.N. interest, the politically conservative imperial governments which held sway most of the time in post-war Europe, would have, in all likelihood, continued to be insensitive to the growing discontent of their colonial peoples.

Another contribution which the U.N. made to African nationalism deserves special attention because of the role of India. In 1947, two years after the U.N. was born, India won its independence and was elected to the organization. Once in the U.N., India immediately assumed leadership of the Afro-Asian bloc of nations and led the fight for decolonization.

Taking U.N. operations as a whole, no part of its machinery was closer to the nationalist ferment in Africa than the Trusteeship Council. This was because the U.N. Charter, in replacing and liberalizing the Mandate system of the old League of Nations, provided for an International Trusteeship System for the administration and supervision of Trusteeship governments.

7

Toward this end, the Trusteeship Council was established as one of the principal organs of the U.N. to look after the interests of the various territorial peoples, most of whom were in Africa. This involved the Council in the daily affairs of all seven African Trust Territories, of which all but one, Italian Somaliland, were former Mandate Territories.

In order to carry out this task the Trusteeship Council was instructed by the Charter:

> to promote the political, economic, social, and educational advancement of the inhabitants of the Trust Territories, and their progressive development towards self-government or independence as may be appropriate to . . . the freely expressed wishes of the peoples concerned.

To accomplish this purpose the Council was authorized to consider annual reports submitted by special representatives of the Administering Authority in each Trust Territory. It was also empowered to accept petitions and to receive and listen to African petitioners in person. Most important of all, there was provision for periodic visits to each territory by inspecting U.N. Visiting Missions, whose personnel was drawn from among the Council members. Information from these sources formed the basis of the reports which the Council was required to submit annually for final disposition by the General Assembly.

During the 1950's, the Council itself consisted of 14 members divided equally between members representing nations with administering authority over one or more Territories and those without such authority. In 1953, when I first took a seat, the Administering Authorities included Great Britain for Tanganyika and its parts of Togoland and the Cameroons; France for its parts of Togoland and the Cameroons; Belgium for Ruanda-Urundi; Italy for Italian Somaliland; Australia for New Guinea and Nauru; New Zealand for Western Samoa; and the U.S. for those islands scattered all over the Pacific which it had captured from the Japanese during World War II. The non-administering members included India, the Soviet Union, nationalist China or Taiwan, Syria, El Salvador, Guatemala and Haiti.

Except in the case of the United States, almost all the representatives of the Administering Authorities were former colonial governors with wide experience and a profound knowledge of the areas in which they served. Great Britain was represented by Sir Alan Burns, former governor of the Gold Coast and Acting Governor-General of Nigeria. His position in representing Great Britain was ambiguous. He was very outspoken in his delight over the approaching independence of the Gold Coast, to be renamed Ghana. At the same time, he was a determined advocate for the continuation of colonial administration of Tanganyika in East Africa. Sir Alan was also plainly anti-American, in part due to his irritation with the anti-colonial mood of the American public.

Representing Belgium was Pierre Ryckmans, a brilliant former Governor-General of the Belgian Congo. The welfare of the Congo and its continuation as a colony was for him almost a religion and it is perhaps fortunate that he died just before a politically unprepared Congo assumed its independence amid a period of violence and hatred.

Among the non-administering members was Krishna Menon of India. Menon was very close to Pandit Nehru, first Prime Minister of India, and had been imprisoned with him by the British during the final days before independence. Perhaps it was this imprisonment or memories of inconsiderate treatment at the hands of the British that caused him to develop a passion against any presumption of white superiority.

The effects on the proceedings of a Council divided between representatives of the imperial nations and representatives of those nations which had once been under colonial rule was predictable. Although the business of the Council was concerned solely with matters coming under enlightened U.N. trusteeship, the basic core issue was colonialism and how soon foreign rule could be replaced by home rule. It was an issue which allowed little room for any compromise. The one nation which might have taken a conciliatory course was the United States. As the first colony to win its independence and well-known for its support of self-determination, it was ideally qualified to play an "honest broker" role for the benefit of both sides. But for reasons to be examined in succeeding chapters this was not to be the case. As a result, without the intervention of a moderating United States influence, the work of the Council was bound to become a series of virtually unending debate during which the non-administering members subjected the administering members to critical cross-examinations of conditions in their respective territories and the administering members fought back.

Also of great interest and importance were the frequent appearances before the Council of African celebrities who came to New York to testify about their homelands. These visitors were almost always prominent nationalist leaders, some of whom, like Julius Nyerere of Tanganyika, Sylvanus Olympio of Togoland, and Aden Abdulah Osman of Somalia, were destined to become the first presidents or prime ministers of their independent nations. The fact that they appeared before the U.N. added new prestige to their names and increased attention to their views, both abroad and at home.

Most important of all to the decolonization process was the authority of the Council to dispatch Visiting Missions to conduct on-the-spot inspections of each Trust Territory and to render reports on their findings, which usually commanded wide international attention.

There were numerous reasons for this. In the first place, these Missions by definition of the Charter were U.N. Missions, not Missions of U.N. member states. Secondly, they were usually comprised of four members selected from among the Council delegations, two from the Administering Authorities and two from the non-Administering Authorities. Thirdly, as already noted, the Charter of the U.N. and more particularly the specific provisions setting forth the purposes of the Trusteeship Council, were essentially anti-colonial in nature. Moreover, the supporting personnel which the Secretary-General of the U.N. assigned to assist each Mission consisted of secretariat people. These, of course, were U.N. "civil servants," devoted to the U.N. Charter and its philosophies. Among this group were territorial specialists on each of the territories to be visited. Their duty was to keep a diary of the Mission's travels, to record the views of Mission members as well as the information which was obtained from Africans interviewed during innumerable hearings, and upon returning to New York to prepare the first working drafts of the Mission's report.

This draft was then discussed, paragraph by paragraph, with the Mission until, after much work, the final report and its recommendations were in shape for the approval of the Council and U.N. General Assembly. Since the non-Administering members of each Mission were invariably of anti-colonial disposition, dissenting views could be raised only if either of the two members of the administering side desired strongly enough to insert objections into the report itself. But since unanimous reports were obviously more seriously considered and more likely to be accepted than those with divided views, a pride of Mission would more often than not influence the objectors to agree to a compromise which could be reworded in such a way that it would be accepted by the anti-colonial members and become a unanimous document.

Thus, by the very nature, the process of evaluation tended to favor the forces of decolonization and stimulated the member states to pick up the pace of eventual self rule.

Chapter II

Africa in Ferment

In the early 1950's there was a considerable reservoir of good will in Africa towards the United States. Unfortunately, John Foster Dulles did not continue to express the traditional sympathy of our country towards self-determination of peoples. Because of the cold war, he decided to subordinate the promotion of African freedom to what he considered the overriding necessity to support our NATO allies and their colonial policies. Yet, while Mr. Dulles was establishing this policy, events in Africa were indicating that nationalism and a desire for independence were widespread and profoundly felt.

In December, 1952, a few months before I went to work at the U.N., there was a tragic outbreak of labor riots in Casablanca, Morocco. These lasted an entire week before French troops were able to restore order. Over a thousand Moroccans and French were killed. A state of emergency was declared throughout the country, and the Istiqlal, the Independence Party, was outlawed and its affiliated newspapers suspended. But unrest continued.

Eight months later, State Department cables coming to the U.S. Mission at the U.N. reported that mounting tensions in Morocco had become so great that it was feared there might be a general massacre of Europeans. The French authorities thereupon decided to engineer the abdication of Sultan Mohammed V and exile him to Corsica. The abdication was a dramatic operation in which the Sultan's great enemy, the French-supported El Glaoui, anti-nationalist Pasha of Marrakech. and ruler of the Berber tribes of the Atlas Mountains, called thousands of his famous cavalrymen down to the plains and massed them before Rabat, the capital city, ostensibly to prevent bloodshed, but in reality to pull off a *coup*; the French army was quickly ordered to surround the Royal Palace. From there the Sultan was taken at pistol point to the airport. He and his family were then flown to exile, first in Corsica and later in Madagascar.

This turned out to be a blunder of major proportions. Sidi Mohammed, the deposed Sultan, was replaced by Moulay ben Arafa, a puppet Sultan who had no influence whatever with the mass of the Moroccan people. The result was that Sidi Mohammed became a martyr, so idolized by the people he had left behind that they refused even to enter their mosques, since they were no longer permitted to pray for their former ruler. Meanwhile, all the Istiqlal leaders either escaped from the country or were imprisoned. Disorder and violence continued until Morocco eventually won its independence.

The turmoil which accompanied the closing days of colonialism in Morocco was also occurring in both Tunisia and Algeria. In Tunisia it became clear, by early 1952, that the people intended to have their independence, and the Bey of Tunis appealed to the U.N. for support. When requested by the French to withdraw this appeal and keep it out of the U.N., the Bey refused, thus precipitating a chain of events which had uncalculated consequences. The French Resident General immediately ordered the army to undertake punitive measures which resulted in the loss of many Tunisian lives. At the same time, the Neo Destour, the Independence Party of Tunisia, was banned and its leaders arrested. These included Habib Bourgiba, a respected and able leader, soon to be the first President of a sovereign Tunisia. Bourgiba's influence was such that the French found it necessary to exile him. It was the fourth time Bourgiba had been forcibly removed from the political life of his country. His place was taken over by the No. 2 Nationalist, Ferhat

Hached, a labor executive who was well-known to American labor. But Hached's leadership was tragically cut short when he was slain by members of a secret society of European settlers known as the Red Hand. The assassination of Mr. Hached not only brought on costly labor riots a few days later, but gave rise to a period of unrest and violence between terrorist Moslem bands and European vigilantes. This terror continued into 1954, until the government of Pierre Mendes-France eased matters by lifting the ban on the Neo Destour and negotiating with Tunisians for internal self-government. This came in June of 1955, less than a year before Tunisia was to assume total independence.

Meanwhile, the situation deteriorated even further in Algeria. During 1945, there had been a fearful killing of Europeans as local guerrilla groups advocating Algerian independence went on a rampage. Over 100 Europeans were killed. In retaliation, the French killed thousands of Moslems and put thousands more into prison.

Shortly after the 1945 insurrection, a small group of Algerian Nationalists organized an underground movement based on an outlawed party, the Algerian Peoples Party. By 1953, these "shock groups," which went under the name of the Special Organization, had become a secret terrorist army of great destructive capability. It was under the command of a small general staff of nine men headed by Ahmed Ben Bella, one of the most prominent Nationalist leaders. In preparation for the rebellion, this group had organized a network of hidden supply depots which contained machine guns, rifles, pistols, explosives, medical equipment, and instruction manuals.

When the rebellion broke out on November 1, 1954, neither the European *colons* in Algeria nor the government in Paris were prepared for what happened. The case of Algeria was further clouded by the thinking of the professional military of that period, both in Europe and the U.S., which had concluded that colonialism in Africa was not of too great a concern in comparison with the far greater importance which they attached to the NATO defense

15

against the Russians in Europe.

 With the unforeseen outbreak of the Algerian rebellion, the serious and far-reaching political misjudgements of the 1950's began. It should have become perfectly clear at this moment that a colonial system based on racial domination could no longer be maintained by force. In Algeria, the rebellion date was so carefully planned and the element of surprise so carefully guarded that the orders for commencing the attacks were not issued by the rebel command until October 31, 1954. Early the next morning terrorist attacks took place simultaneously at seventy points all over the country, marking the beginning of the end of French authority over Algeria. Although it was at first the operation of a small, well-organized army of terrorists, it immediately pointed out the danger that France might have to fight on the whole of North Africa at the same time. This was one reason why the French government soon accepted the possibility of granting independence for both Morocco and Tunisia.

 Added to the burdens which its colonial empire was saddling on France, was the dramatic defeat six months earlier of a sorely pressed French army at Dien Bien Phu in Indo-China. This defeat marked the last chapter of the long, 7½-year war, which had been killing thousands of soldiers on both sides, including the bulk of the Officer Corps graduating annually from Saint Cyr, the French counterpart of West Point.

 It is pertinent here to glimpse General Eisenhower's thinking on the war in Indo-China. In his memoirs, written while he was still in command of the NATO forces in Europe, he stated that among the conditions which he had deemed necessary before the NATO allies would consider military assistance to the French in Indo-China, were, there would have to be a definite and public pledge on the part of the French to accord independence and the right of self-determination to the Indo-Chinese as soon as military victory was attained. He then added that he had "repeatedly urged upon successive French governments the wisdom of publishing to the Free World and particularly to all Indo-China such an unequivocal commitment." He further observed that:

in the absence of such a statement the war was naturally looked upon in most cases as a domestic difficulty between France and one part of their empire [and that] this attitude precluded the possibility that other free nations could help in what the French themselves considered so much a family quarrel that it could not even be submitted to the U.N. for adjudication.

Again, after Eisenhower had become President, he asserted that the:

willingness to fight for freedom, no matter where the battle may be, has always been characteristic of our people, but the conditions then prevailing [in 1954] in Indo-China were such as to make unilateral American intervention nothing less than sheer folly.

Yet, President Eisenhower was virtually alone in this opinion. Vice President Nixon, Secretary Dulles and Admiral Radford, all urged the President to intervene on behalf of France. Secretary Dulles and Vice President Nixon even went so far as to recommend the use of nuclear weapons.

The loss of Indo-China in 1954 compounded the crisis facing France in North Africa and made it abundantly clear that she could no longer maintain control over her vast overseas empire. At the same time that the failures of French colonial policy were attracting world-wide attention, the former empire of Italy in Libya and Somalia was coming peacefully to an end. This occurred because both countries were placed under U.N. supervision with a guarantee of independence at a specific date.

Libya came under U.N. supervision in 1949 and by 1950 was notified that independence would come at the end of 1951. The case of Libya was particularly interesting because under every rule laid down by most colonial administrators, this land should have

17

been one of the last countries to attain independence in the whole of Africa.

Its people were determined to have independence, however. After the First World War, during which Libyans pushed the Italians into the coastal towns, the Italian government signed a treaty granting Libya independence. But the Italian Parliament refused to ratify the agreement. This led to nearly ten years more of fighting until the commander of the Senussi forces in Cyrenaica was captured by the Italians and hung. In World War II, Sayyid Mohammed Idris, later to become Sultan of all Libya, joined with the Allies to defeat the Axis in North Africa.

When independence came in 1951, however, Libya had little or no assets with which to better the lot of its people. It was an enormous country with desert areas larger than Western Europe. It had no fresh water except in the wells of a few widely separated oases. With only about 2% of its land in production and a *per capita* income as little as ten cents a day, it was one of the most impoverished countries in the world, requiring much of its population to live close to starvation.

On top of this, there were less than 20 university graduates available to join in organizing a sovereign government. Under the circumstances, this new nation was at first unable to support itself without the outside aid, both financial and technical, which came to it from Great Britain and the U.S. in return for rights to military bases. However, the discovery of oil soon brought in more money than the government could spend. This created a sharp rise in the living standards of many people with the prospects of further increases as time went on. Although Libya suddenly became able to stand on its own financially, the advent of an oil industry required great numbers of technical advisors, which came not only from Europe, the U.S. and the U.N., but also from Egypt and the Near East.

By the middle sixties, the oil windfall had changed the face of Libya. Where education had been almost non-existent a system of national primary and secondary schools was developed. Attendance was compulsory and the teaching staffs were manned increasingly by Libyans.

Many other aspects of Libyan progress might be cited, but the point here is that the discovery of oil gave a powerful push to Libyan development. Equally important was the fact that the Libyan people were capable of making and presiding over the educational and material progress which came to their country almost overnight. While this would have been impossible without massive foreign technical assistance, the Libyan record underlines the abilities which reside in all peoples if they are given a fair chance and proper assistance. While this observation may appear simple-minded, it is necessary to make it because mental and human potential of relatively uneducated societies were greatly underrated during much of colonial history. Almost all African leaders argued that people in developing societies were capable of educating themselves and modernizing their economies fully after independence.

The Trust Territory of Somalia on the Horn of North East Africa was like Libya in many respects. An Italian colony, it was liberated by a British army in World War II. A few years later, on April 1, 1950, in agreement with the U.N., Somalia was placed under International Trusteeship and assigned to Italian Government administration, with the proviso that it would become independent on April 1, 1960. The fixing of a target date for independence did much to keep the particularly volatile politics in Somalia from exploding.

Another instance of the setting of target dates for independence occurred in the early days of Mr. Dulles' secretaryship, in February, 1953, when agreement was reached between Great Britain and Egypt, promising the Sudan internal self-government in November of that year and the right to vote on independence in 1956. The Sudan had a long history of nationalism. This was particularly true for the northern Islamic half of the Sudan.

In sharp contrast to those countries where independence had already been granted or was scheduled for a specific date in the future, a critical situation was developing in British East Africa, where it was feared by the Africans that there might be attempts to maintain colonialism indefinitely. This was

19

particularly the case in both Kenya and Uganda, where there was widespread fear that the white settlers would insist on the longest possible period of colonial rule.

In Kenya, dislike of entrenched white rule brought on the so-called "Mau Mau" uprising in late 1952. The Mau Mau Rebellion caught the government off balance and showed how much damage could be inflicted upon white authority even by a small number of resentful men. These Mau Mau units were made up primarily of Kikuyus, the largest and most powerful tribe in Kenya and the one which had had most contact with the settler community.

If the Mau Mau uprising was an abnormal manifestation of nationalism in Africa, there were other Kenyan developments which were very similar to events in other colonies and protectorates. Although the Mau Mau uprising captured world-wide attention, there was already a well-defined and effective nationalist movement headed by Jomo Kenyatta, the future president of Kenya and one of the most famous political leaders of Africa. In the earliest days of the Mau Mau, he was called upon by the British to use his great influence to call off the terrorists. He tried and failed and in the tensions of the moment was arrested, put on trial and convicted as the principal instigator of the movement. He was then sentenced to what amounted to permanent exile in the far northern wastelands of Kenya. From start to finish, the manner of holding the trial, its removal from Nairobi to a remote spot hundreds of miles away, as well as the admission and subsequent repudiation of evidence, led many Europeans and unbiased observers from the outside to believe that Mr. Kenyatta had been falsely accused and was innocent of the charge against him. As might have been expected, Kenyatta's exile only served to increase his stature.

While the Mau Mau Rebellion was attracting growing international attention to Kenya in 1953, another government crisis involving political exile was building up for the British in neighboring Uganda. From a colonial viewpoint, Uganda was a model state. There was no large community of white settlers because the British government did not permit white ownership of land. In consequence, white supremacy had not been as humiliating an experience as it had been in so many other parts of Africa. The cause of the crisis was an injudicious remark made in London in June, 1953, by the Conservative Colonial Secretary, Sir Oliver Lyttleton, suggesting that the three territories of British East Africa, Uganda, Tanganyika and Kenya, might be federated one day.

The thought of permanent East African domination by Kenya, where the white-settler community was in control, was too much for the Africans. It reminded them of what had happened two months earlier when the Protectorates of Northern Rhodesia and Nyasaland and the colony of Southern Rhodesia were incorporated by the British Parliament into the Central African Federation, thus placing them under the domination of the white settlers, who controlled the government of Southern Rhodesia. It was more than Africans could accept. This was especially true in Buganda, by far the largest and most powerful state in Uganda, where the Kabaka, its traditional ruler, promptly demanded not only independence for his people, but a specific target date for its attainment. This, of course, would have meant the end of the British effort to build Uganda into a workable federation with Buganda as the core around which to assemble the three remaining states.

This unforeseen demand for Bugandan independence faced the British government with a most difficult dilemma. As a practical problem of colonial politics, the British authority could not survive if it gave in to the Kabaka and his well-established government, for the Kabaka was determined to abrogate the original treaty with Great Britain under which the Protectorate of greater Uganda was established. Instead, the British hastened to send the Kabaka into exile. In many ways, it was similar to the sudden removal by France of the Sultan of Morocco. Like the French action, it also failed. Because of his exile, the Kabaka gained a political standing all over Uganda which he had never before enjoyed. Upon his return in 1955, the Kabaka was treated as a hero.

A rollcall of the famous political prisoners that will go down in the history of African independence must include the Sultan of Morocco, Habib Bourgiba of Tunisia, Kwame Nkrumah of the Gold Coast (now Ghana), Jomo Kenyatta of Kenya, Hastings Banda of Nyasaland (now Malawi), Kenneth Kaunda of Northern Rhodesia (now Zambia), the Kabaka of Uganda and many more. That most of these leaders should have been imprisoned during the early 1950's was particularly significant. In the first place, in the minds of millions of their followers, the mere act of the colonial governments in trying to remove their influence from the political arena was tantamount to recognizing the contribution they were making to the future independence of their countries. And, secondly, remembering the countries of Asia, where independence came swiftly following the imprisonment of leaders such as Ghandi and Nehru, the similar imprisonment of so many prominent African leaders was widely interpreted as an indication that the end of the colonial era was nearer than expected.

Had the Colonial Offices of Europe entertained a deeper curiosity and a more timely and human understanding of nationalist leadership as it developed in all the African colonies, it might have been able to diminish the violence which accompanied the closing days of colonialism. In the U.S., especially, if the State Department had shown a greater desire to learn more about the caliber of these leaders and what they were thinking, it could have been a significant influence in persuading Mr. Dulles to adopt a more sympathetic policy toward African self-determination. Unfortunately, no such interest was evident, at least among the senior professional diplomats of the Department.

At the heart of the colonial system was the doctrine of white supremacy. It was assumed that Europeans knew what was best for their colonial charges and that Africans had much to learn from their rulers. This element of racism in the colonial experience caused deep-seated resentment on the part of the individuals who faced it on a daily basis.

Even today, white supremacy is a difficult thing to discuss because of the emotional reactions which it still arouses in so many people, be they black or white. Perhaps a feeling of white superiority was inevitable when the mechanical know-how of the industrial West began to penetrate into Africa. But it went far beyond this as Europeans asserted the primacy of their entire culture over that of the Africans.

One of the most penetrating analyses of the struggle between white supremacy and African nationalism is that of Reverend Ndabaningi Sithole, who was jailed in Rhodesia because of his opposition to white domination. Dr. Sithole rightly suggests that:

There is a sense in which 'white supremacy' may be regarded as having been largely responsible for the effective cross-fertilization of African nationalism. Without the existence of the racially biased doctrine of 'white supremacy,' which adversely affected the African peoples, it is probable that the African peoples would not have sensed so quickly the 'consciousness of kind' which boomeranged on the colonial powers and the white settlers.

Reverend S. Tule observes that when the white man first arrived in Africa he came as a conqueror and that "the conqueror attitude always tends to downgrade the humanity of the conquered [although] in fairness to the white people, it should be pointed out that it is not only they who tend to look at other people in this fashion. It is a universal trait among all conquerors regardless of the color of their skins, their creeds and nationalities."

Dr. Sithole argues that the European contention that Africans were perfectly happy under European rule is nonsense and he cites the many instances of African armed resistance: the Ashanti wars against the British in the 19th century, the so-called Kaffir wars between European settlers and the Xhosa tribe in South Africa, the Matabele and Mashona rebellions against the British in Rhodesia, and the Mau Mau rebellion in East Africa.

With Dr. Sithole's views in mind, one can imagine the feelings which white supremacy aroused in the Africans with university backgrounds. Educated as they were in the Western traditions of human liberty, including the revolutionary histories of

23

the colonial powers themselves, it became impossible for these men to accept life for themselves and their people as second-class citizens in their own lands.

The tragedy of American foreign policy during this era is that it did not appreciate the extent of African opposition to white racism and the colonial experience. Nor did it take into account the worldwide striving to attain political independence, a striving that was so much a part of the American Revolution itself.

Watching dancers during 1954 East Africa Trip

Arrival of Sears Mission in Lamu, Kenya

Chapter III

Mission to West Africa

In 1954, I was authorized to visit the Belgian Congo (now Zaïre), Nigeria, the British and French Cameroons, British and French Togoland, and the Gold Coast (now Ghana). We flew into Leopoldville (now Kinshasa), capital of the Belgian Congo, over Stanley Pool, where the famous explorer ended his adventurous journey across the continent.

It is always an inspiring sight to come into Leopoldville from the air; to look down on its skyscrapers and the river shipping tied up at the docks; and to think of what the great Congo River, flowing for 1000 navigable miles through the interior, will carry when the wealth of central Africa is fully opened up to international commerce.

If one were to sum up Belgian colonial policy in a phrase, it would be "economic development". The heart of that development is the city of Leopoldville with its office buildings and banks, its restaurants and stores, its wide avenues and motor cars. Leopoldville was both a modern European metropolis and a sprawling African city. All over Africa the community marketplaces are filled with interest not only for what they sell but because of the crowds of people they attract and, in these regards, the Leopoldville market was truly impressive.

Proof of Leopoldville's prosperity was evident in the

growth of its population, which was said to have increased from about 100,000 to 300,000 people from the end of World War II until 1954. To accommodate these newcomers, the Belgian authorities were expanding the city's outskirts by erecting more and more low-cost, two-room housing units which extended, like military barracks, in long lines across the open plain.

The plans which Belgium had for the future of the Congo and the Belgian Trust Territory of Ruanda-Urundi were outlined in an interview we had which Bob McGregor, the very able American Consul-General at Leopoldville, arranged for me with Governor-General Petillon. The Governor-General was a short, friendly man who had spent many years in the Belgian colonial service. Before coming to Leopoldville, he had been Governor of Ruanda-Urundi, a territory to which he had become much attached. He remarked that he had left his heart with its people and its hills and also said that he had not wanted to undertake the responsibilities of Governor-General of the Congo, but he made it clear that he had complete confidence in the wisdom of Belgian colonial policy, and especially in the current ten year plan, which he had helped to devise. Like most Belgian colonial officials, he obviously had a sincere personal affection for the Congolese people.

As outlined to me, Belgian policy was based on a belief that one day, in conjunction with an emancipated Congolese people and their expanding wealth, a huge united Belgian-Congolese Community could become one of the world's greatest powers. It was a dream of heroic proportions to which the Belgian Government was totally dedicated and about which it was extremely sensitive and understandably resistant to criticism. But, like so many other colonial assumptions it had a fatal flaw: the Belgians were misreading the temper of Africa by believing they had generations in which to achieve their goal.

In 1954, however, when I was privileged to call upon Governor-General Petillon, Belgium was confident that its particular brand of colonialism was the one most likely to succeed. It was soon clear that Belgian preoccupation with the Congo was due, in part, to the fact that the economy of the colony was so interwoven with the economy of the *metropole* that, instead of the Congo being dependent on Belgium, as would normally be the case, it was Belgium that was dependent on the Congo.

Therefore, it was not surprising, though it was ill-advised, that the government took strict measures to prevent anything that might encourage the emergence of nationalism in the Congo. That was why the colonial administration maintained a repressive military force and permitted no one in the Congo, black or white, to enjoy any political rights. Through these measures, the Belgians hoped to insure tranquility in the Congo and, with the assistance of the Catholic Church, gradually to provide a standard of education for the whole mass of the Congolese people which would compare favorably with the most literate societies in other parts of the world. It was a bold policy even though it was inevitably tinged with too much paternalism and suffered from the political miscalculations which made it incapable of resisting the tide of nationalism that was soon to sweep in and bring it to a violent end.

Across the river from Leopoldville, on the other side of Stanley Pool, was the city of Brazzaville, capital of what was then called the French Congo. In terms of atmosphere no two cities could be more different. In place of the hustle of Leopoldville there was an air of relaxation, an easy-going atmosphere in which even the French part of the city seemed to submerge itself into a purely African setting. But if they fitted into the life of Africa on the spot, the French never forgot for one moment that, for them, the one and only culture worth emulation was that of France. It was their view that they were doing a favor to the African people in trying to assimilate them into the French attitude toward life. Since there was less snobbery in the French attitude, less constant evidence of irritating personal superiority, as was prevalent in all other white settler communities in Africa, many Africans were assimilated into French culture. As a result, some Africans married French women, who accompanied them back to Africa. Many more Africans became officers in the French Army. Some became members of the French Parliament and several became members of French cabinets. Some among the most famous of these became the fathers of their countries, including

Bourgiba in Tunisia, Senghor in Senegal, and Houphouet-Boigny in the Ivory Coast.

However, any policy based on assimilation of overseas peoples into distant non-African culture ultimately meant nothing less than the ultimate racial subordination of the Africans. As such, assimilation was certain to fail. The French, like the Belgians, thought they had the answer to the evolution of colonialism, something that would be at once good for France and acceptable to their colonies. The trouble was that the nationalism which was beginning to emerge in many parts of Africa, especially in French North Africa, was incompatible with the French policy of assimilation.

Soon after arriving in Africa, I was present at an occasion which demonstrated the kind of political progress that French policy was encouraging in its Black African colonies. It took place at Fort Fourreau, an important community situated at the northern tip of the Trust Territory of French Cameroon. The occasion was the installation of the first African to succeed a Frenchman as a regional administrator, a post which was responsible for the welfare of thousands of African families. My son and I and our companion, Bill Drew, U.S. Vice Consul from Leopoldville, were invited to join the new administrator and a group of French officials in reviewing the installation ceremonies.

The celebration had attracted a large crowd, including the most eminent African personages from miles around. At the center of attention were three high-ranking Muslim chiefs, called *Lamidos* by the French, or *Emirs* by the British. These potentates, spaced at intervals around the edges of the ceremonial enclosure, were sitting under their huge multicolored royal umbrellas, around which were collected retainers, groups of young palace women, drummers, and high notables astride horses protected by ancient armor.

Finally, when all was ready and the ceremonies were about to begin, I was directed to a seat under the reviewing tent, next to the incoming chief of the Region, who invited me to join him in the inspection of an honor guard which was drawn up in the center of the arena. After that, the horsemen left the area *en masse*, but soon returned from a side entrance to pass in review in groups of four to eight mounted notables, each accompanied by a retinue of numerous drummers and horn blowers on foot. After they had all passed by, there was an interim period during which I was taken around to be introduced to the *Lamidos*.

Soon, the horsemen made a dramatic reappearance. This time, each group formed in a front and raced by at full gallop, some with swords thrust forward as if attacking an enemy, others with spears which they threw high into the air and caught again without slowing down. At the end of the charge, in one final tense moment, they would rein in their horses at the edge of the arena and come to a full stop, so abruptly that the animals would rear up on their hindquarters with their forefeet flailing the air in the very faces of the frightened spectators.

Following the ceremonies at Fort Fourreau, we were met by a senior official of the French government, Monsieur Tirant, who came to escort us in the High Commissioner's airplane. Throughout our travels we were treated very courteously and hospitably by the French.

For the next few days, we flew to several of the cities in the Muslim sections of the country. At each of these we called upon the Regional *Lamidos* so that I could pay my respects and indicate the interest of the U.S. in their people. Although their palatial residences were much the same, we had a particularly interesting visit with the *Lamido* who resided in Ngoundéré, one of the larger cities of the Cameroons. His residence comprised a series of mud-walled houses firmly built and covered with well-thatched roofs. A live peacock was perched on the peak of one. The houses themselves were connected by a labyrinth of courtyards and passageways surrounded by a wall of thatch.

It is one thing to imagine the pomp and ceremony of strange places and bygone times. But it is quite another thing when one is suddenly and physically transplanted back through the ages. Yet, that was the way it was when we entered the palace. In reality, it was the past.

Like the *Lamido* of Garua, all of the *Lamidos* we
visited were chieftains who held nearly absolute power over their
people. Reinforced by the disciplines of the Muslim faith and backed
by followers who were warriors by tradition, they were masters in
their own lands and, therefore, somewhat immunized from the
effects of white supremacy.

To a lesser degree, many of the traditional chiefs
among the non-Muslim tribes of French areas were also
conservative. These men were catered to by the French colonial
authorities and enjoyed a privileged status which the French used to
offset the growing influence of nationalist groups. Here again,
among these favored chiefs there was an obvious African affinity
with certain phases of French culture. This affinity appeared to have
more to do with easy human relations and the gracious side of French
living than anything else.

Yet, the political situation which was developing in
urban areas like Lomé in Togo was in sharp contrast to the feelings of
the village chiefs. Like all French-designed cities in West Africa,
Lomé was a very attractive tropical community with its broad, tree-
lined avenues and streets, clean white government buildings and
well-shaded residences, all close by beautiful sandy beaches.
Although I was carefully shielded while visiting the city from any but
French influence, I learned later that nationalist leaders of several
parties had tried repeatedly to arrange for meetings with me, but had
been prevented by the French police from doing so.

One instance in particular gave me concern. This was
the failure of being allowed to meet with Sylvanus Olympio, who was
then the leading nationalist. He eventually became a very good friend
of mine and one whom I greatly admired. Destined to become the
father of his country and its first President, Olympio was one of those
outstanding individuals about whom much will be written when the
history of African independence is fully recorded. His tragic death by
assassination cut short a brilliant and dedicated career of public
service.

When my son and I visited the French High
Commissioner of the Togo Trust Territory, he informed me that Mr.

Olympio had lost much ground politically and was no longer of any real influence. Looking back, it obviously was a political stratagem of the French to downgrade Mr. Olympio so that I would not bring back a favorable opinion of him when I returned to the Trusteeship Council in New York. At the time, the French had their own puppet leader, Mr. Grunitsky, who himself was to become President some time after Mr. Olympio's death.

Curiously enough, Mr. Grunitsky was the brother-in-law of Mr. Olympio. In spite of this family relationship, when the Togolese people finally voted in a U.N.-supervised election to make Sylvanus Olympio their first President— thereby disregarding the views of African tribal chiefs and French administrators—Mr. Grunitsky and his French-supported associates fled to France for safety.

In marked contrast to French colonial policy, the policy of the British in West Africa was, in some ways, so much more politically liberal as to be almost breath-taking by comparison. Unlike all the other colonial powers in Africa, Great Britain's basic goal was the full freedom of its colonies—albeit at some distant moment in time. The British ambition, which was far more realistic than those of the other powers, was to evolve its huge empire into a commonwealth of free, sovereign nations. The turning point, so far as its Afro-Asian Empire was concerned, came in 1947 and 1948, when it recognized the independence of India, Pakistan, Ceylon and Burma. The genuineness of this action was emphasized when Burma, on its own, chose to remain independent of even an association with the Commonwealth.

As long as 25 years before Indian independence, the direction of some government thinking in London was indicated by an official white paper which set a moral tone toward colonialism. In this early declaration, the wording of which was to be used later with shrewd effect by the Nationalist movement in the Trust Territory of Tanganyika, it was emphasized in plain and considered language that the colony of Kenya, in spite of its politically and economically influential white settlers was "primarily . . . an African Territory in which the interests of the African people not only 'must be

31

paramount' but specifically senior to European settler interests should any conflict with them arise." The declaration went on to say, in words and tone which was strikingly prophetic of the U.N. Charter, that the British government considered its presence and purposes in Kenya to be that of a trustee on behalf of the "protection and advancement" of the African people.

This idealistic approach was destined to become progressively diluted, mainly because the conservative Tory Governments in London refused to become committed to any definite timing for the accomplishment of political progress. This meant that the pace of progress could be so slowed down that the spirit of the 1923 declaration would be rendered meaningless. In other words, the march toward future independence could be spread out over one hundred years or at such a leisurely pace as to mean little less than holding a colony in perpetual bondage. This, in fact, was the hope of many people, particularly in British East Africa, where the Colonial administrators ultimately refused to have anything to do with timetables or long-range target dates for independence. Just as Indian independence was the signal which precipitated the far-flung transition from an Empire with colonies to a Commonwealth of free nations in Asia, so the speed of political progress in British West Africa, where Ghana was on the verge of independence, was the counterpart in Africa that precipitated the wave of final independence.

The disparities between British colonial policies in East and West Africa were so marked that it was hard to think of them as emanating from the same government. They illustrated the flexibility of the British approach to two vastly different colonial problems. In West Africa, the problem of independence was complicated by tribal differences. It was largely a case of Africans *versus* Africans, with the conservative, less sophisticated tribes of the interior resisting the domination of the more politically minded tribes along the coast.

In East Africa, on the other hand, the promotion of independence was essentially a racial struggle, a case of Europeans *versus* Africans. The problem here centered entirely in the opposition of the European settlers in Kenya, who had established a successful agricultural economy. The benefits of this economy were mostly restricted to the cities and farming communities in which the Europeans lived. They did not reach the Africans in the countryside beyond. As a result, the ideals of the British White Paper of 1923 had been largely discarded by 1954, in favor of a movement toward white-settler nationalism which had an obvious political impact on the government in London.

To an outsider, far from the confidences of the inner councils in London, it looked as if the Colonial Office was hypersensitive to settler hostility and simply too anxious not to upset their interests. By way of illustration, in Nairobi during 1953, the British governor of Kenya, Sir Evelyn Baring, was besieged in his residence in Government House by an angry mob of British settlers following the brutal murder of a white-settler farming family by a Mau Mau group. Even though this very dangerous settler protest involved a seemingly justifiable European call upon the Governor to provide more adequate security measures against the Mau Mau terrorists, the startling fact was that an armed mob of British settlers should have had the temerity to try and intimidate a governor sent out from Great Britain, not only to head their government, but to act as a symbol of the Crown.

In East Africa particularly, the effort to prolong the colonial status while other parts of the continent were reaching the threshold of independence, made such a policy not only difficult but dangerous. It was a great mistake, for example, for the colonial administrators of white-settler areas to believe they could persuade African political leaders to agree peacefully to defer their demands for independence on the ground that they were unprepared to sustain it if it came. From an African viewpoint, if they were short of trained administrative personnel at first, this could be corrected rather quickly.

By contrast, British policy in West Africa, where there were few white settlers, recognized the inevitability of independence and encouraged progress toward it. Since the right hand knew what the left was doing, at least in the colonial office in London, it was curious that their colonial representatives in East Africa appeared to be so unprepared for the political impact which the early arrival of self-government in West Africa was certain to have throughout the entire continent.

In Nigeria, which we visited after leaving the Cameroons, there was no mistaking the direction of British policy. It was apparent everywhere that independence was to be granted just as soon as the British administrators could persuade the people of the northern Muslim hinterland to throw aside their reluctance to join politically with the two great tribal regions of the coast. Here, in a sense, the British had a dream like the Belgians. With the Belgians, the dream was far off in an ultimate unity between the Belgian people and the huge country of the Congo. With the British, however, the dream was of something almost immediate and involved the creation of a great federal entity which would transform Nigeria into a nation with a political and economic potential larger by far than any other nation in Africa. The recent incorporation of the huge subcontinent of India into the British Commonwealth, and then the likelihood that a federated Nigeria would soon be added, made it easy to appreciate what a very powerful commonwealth of free nations was beginning to emerge in place of the old colonial empire of Great Britain.

Lagos was the capital city of the new Nigerian federation which had been authorized by the British Government a few months before our visit. The new constitution encompassed the formation of Federal and regional legislatures in which African political leaders and their followers were given a much greater say in legislation than ever before. This was done in order to prepare the country for the assumption of internal self-government for each of its three great regions by 1956. Complete sovereign independence would follow as soon as the Africans themselves could iron out the problems of their Federal relationships.

For the moment, at least, the Eastern and Western Regions would have liked even faster progress and had been clamoring for full independence by 1956. But the more conservative Muslims of the North were baulking at such speed. The Muslim leaders, like everyone else, looked forward to ending the colonial relationship, but they wanted more time, fearing otherwise that their less-educated people would be swallowed up by the more sophisticated non-Muslims in the coastal regions to the south. Because of this fear, there was great hostility between the northern and southern tribes. To make matters worse, the technical inexperience of the north meant that thousands of southerners, particularly the Ibos, had migrated to the north in order to man the railroads, the post offices and government agencies, all of which required personnel with a standard of education which most Muslims as yet did not possess. Despite the tribal hostilities, the British had undiminished enthusiasm for the approach of an independent federation. Their daring confidence in the future of regional federation for Nigeria, even before the Muslims of the north were agreeable to the idea, was in sharp contrast to the very conservative views toward the possibilities of independence which I found a few months later among the highest colonial officials in British East Africa.

In addition to the political optimism of the British officials and the interest in self-government among Africans in all parts of the country, even in the less progressively-minded north, I was impressed by the historical beauty of the countryside itself, which I am sure affects all new visitors who come to Africa. This was especially true of the great walled city of Kano, a city which was some five hundred years old.

Kano, like Timbuctu, was one of the most important trading centers of northwest Africa. Inside the city walls, and comprising almost a walled city within a city, was the palace and supporting buildings of the Emir of Kano, one of the most powerful Emirs of northern Africa. Our kind British host in Kano arranged for us to call upon the Emir. During the interview, the Emir sat on a special throne while we, his visitors, sat on regular European chairs. On the other side of the Emir were three of his viziers, all of whom were high officials in his government. Toward the end of our conversation, I asked the Emir whether the large northern region was prepared to join the other regions in self-government as promised by the British Colonial Office. He did not answer me directly except to say that his people needed time to "ripen".

Later that day, we took the plane from Kano back to Lagos, where we were met by an aide to Governor-General Macpherson, who drove us in the Governor's car to Government House, where we were to spend the night before our departure for the Gold Coast. That evening, Governor and Lady Macpherson gave us a large formal dinner to which they had invited many of the highest black and white officials in the Nigerian government.

After Nigeria, my son and I travelled to Accra, the capital city of the Gold Coast, where political developments of the greatest significance were in full swing, with implications reaching far beyond the borders of West Africa.

In 1951, the British government had promulgated a new constitution for the Colony, in which it was promised full independence by 1956, as a regular dominion of the Empire, like India, or Canada, or Australia. A year later, in 1952, it was announced that the British government would be pleased to examine any Gold Coast proposals for self-government, a stage just short of independence. In response to this, the African government in Accra reported that it would ask the Gold Coast's National Assembly to debate a motion, certain to be adopted, in which Great Britain would be requested to grant immediate self-government. This was in June of 1953, a year before our arrival.

The report also called for changing the name of Gold Coast to Ghana, and for the replacement of the White members of the cabinet with Africans to make it all African. In due course, this was accepted, leaving the British Governor in control only of the police, the national defense, and foreign affairs. Such was the constitutional background which was in effect during our short stay in this dynamic country. At the time, it represented a rapid political evolution unequalled in any other part of Black Africa.

Along with these constitutional developments was the emergence of Kwame Nkrumah as one of the most politically astute nationalist leaders in Africa. The story of Nkrumah, which began so brilliantly only to end some years later in dismal failure, was remarkable. Without dwelling on his background, which included college educations in both the United States and Great Britain,

Nkrumah returned to his native Gold Coast, where he maneuvered himself into the leadership of a new political party—the Convention Peoples Party (C.P.P.).

In the course of building party membership and promoting a demand for immediate independence, the C.P.P. organized a number of labor strikes and boycotts. In the process, Nkrumah made a series of inflammatory speeches which brought on rioting and looting. As a result, the Governor ordered his arrest and imprisonment. This was early in 1950. A year later, in 1951, following an effective campaign built around a demand for immediate self-government, an election was held for seats in the Colony's Legislature. In this election the C.P.P. won 34 out of a possible 38 seats, including a seat for Nkrumah himself, who had campaigned from prison. Then came a dramatic event in which Governor Sir Charles Arden-Clarke, a greatly admired man who had a deep understanding and high hopes for the future of the Gold Coast people, decided to release Nkrumah from prison so that he could lead the new government of the Colony.

In looking back, it was this period when the U.S. government should have publicly commended both the British and the C.P.P. for the successful manner in which colonialism was being brought to an end in this new emerging nation. Unhappily, little or no recognition was given to this very pivotal situation which was to have such an impact on the rest of Africa.

While we were in Accra, I talked with Prime Minister Nkrumah several times. In the first interview, he was concerned that the Union of South Africa continued to be a member of the British Commonwealth despite its racist policies. The second time we saw Nkrumah was at a political rally of the C.P.P. He put on an impressive display of oratory.

In reporting on my first visit to West Africa, I had to include the problem of the Ewe people who occupied the southern half of British Togoland and part of French Togoland, both of which were Trust Territories coming under the supervision of the United Nation's Trusteeship Council. When the Europeans divided up much of Africa in the 1890's, they drew boundary lines without concern over human geography. The situation was further complicated as the northern, non-Ewe half of British Togoland had long been happily integrated into the northern Territories of the Gold Coast, although it still remained part of the Trust. Ewe reunification had no interest for them. All this created a tug-of-war between the British and the French, in which I found myself in the middle when visiting the two Territories.

The situation abruptly came to a head a few weeks after my son and I left West Africa for home. This happened when the British Government notified the United Nations that, as soon as the Gold Coast attained full independence, it intended to relinquish its responsibility as the Administering Authority. This meant that the Trusteeship Council would be obliged to organize a plebiscite in British Togoland to determine whether the Territory as a whole would vote to go with the British or the French. This was an astute move by the British Government as they knew in advance that the northern peoples would vote on their side and that the French would be forced to concentrate their efforts mainly in the south among the Ewes. Basically, the issue confronting the British half of the Ewe Territory, was whether to go with the Gold Coast, which was to be independent in the near future, or to become associated with the French authorities which had no plans at the time for any sort of independence. Because of this, I later supported the British view in the Trusteeship Council, and there being no objection on the part of the State Department, I did so publicly on behalf of the U.S. Eventually, when the plebiscite was held, the Ewes voted to join with the Gold Coast.

Our visit to West Africa ended at Accra. Although it was a short journey, it had been an eye-opener for me to be in Africa among many and varied peoples; to learn of their ambitions; to observe their economic and political activities; and to be on the spot during the actual birth of new nations. The visit had also been especially valuable to me as it formed a basis for comparison with the conditions which I found later in many parts of Africa.

Chapter IV

Mission to East Africa

Certainly the most controversial of the United Nations Visiting Missions of which I was a member was the one dispatched to East Africa late in 1954. As the representative for the United States, I was joined by Raphael Eguizabel of El Salvador and Rikhi Jaipal of India and John S. Reid of New Zealand, who became our chairperson. Our visits to Ruanda-Urundi, Tanganyika and Italian Somalia set in motion a number of very important decolonization processes. This was due in part to the nature of the Visiting Missions themselves.

The Missions were the nearest thing to direct territorial contact with the outside world. To the Africans, and especially their leaders, these Missions were almost a guarantee that the administering governments abroad would be urged to step up their financial assistance. To the local European officials, Mission visits provided an on-the-spot opportunity to show what was being done to advance the standard of life in their districts. Most of them had reason to be proud of the encouragement they had given to the building of roads, hospitals, schools and the cultivation of the land.

Our first stop was Ruanda-Urundi. Although its land area is very small, approximately the size of Florida, the Belgian Government estimated its rapidly growing population at over four million people, making it the most densely populated region of central Africa. The indigenous population consists mostly of the Hutu people, who comprised 84% of the people. They are agriculturists who, in recent historical times, became dependent on the Tutsi, a pastoral people of remarkably tall and striking physique, who comprise about 15% of the population. The tall Tutsi are of Nilotic origin. The third ethnic group is the Twa, who are very small and make up little more than 1% of the population. There is also a very small European community of about 5,000 people, consisting mainly of government officials and missionaries. There was also a small community of some 2,000 Arab and Indian traders.

The territory was governed through a system of indirect rule, under which the laws were made by the Colonial Administration in Brussels and administered locally by a series of territorial committees. The Belgians maintained strict control through the chiefs which they appointed, and the Tutsi notables who were elected to these Councils by fellow notables.

Although the dimensions of the crises which were soon to take place had not yet emerged, our Mission made a number of observations which, unfortunately, turned out to be accurate:

> The Mission is of the opinion that the rights of the indigenous inhabitants should derive from the status of the Ruanda-Urundi as a trust territory, and not from the laws of the Belgian Congo.
>
> The Mission is disappointed that the Government should have considered it necessary to extend to Ruanda-Urundi certain discriminatory laws and practices of the Belgian Congo which classify indigenous persons into various categories, such as registered civilized persons, civic merit card holders, etc. . . .
>
> The Mission's own impression is that the people of Ruanda-Urundi are inherently intelligent, progressive, and have a great potential for development. The Mission is unable to accept the necessity for them to

be assimilated with non-indigenous persons in a manner followed by the government or in any other manner. Nor can it accept the need for them to be graded among themselves according to the various stages of civilization they may or may not have reached. Such an attitude does grievous injury to human dignity and introduces social discriminations within the indigenous community. Moreover, it gives the impression that in Ruanda-Urundi, equality and human dignity are limited to the civilized few.

The Mission considers that this concept is repugnant to the philosophy of democracy and will endanger human relations in the long run, and possibly also jeopardize the maintenance of peace and order in the Territory.

Mingling among the people of a territory was much more interesting than the Mission's interminable routine of inspecting hospitals, schools, and research outfits arranged for our benefit by the Belgian authorities. There was so much to learn and so little time to do it. But Missions are expensive and are bound by annual schedules set up by the United Nations in New York, which prevents them from being absent too long from headquarters. Our research made it clear that much can be said about the work which the Belgians were doing to help the people raise their standard of living, for economic progress had been excellent and the spectre of famine, which had often plagued the country in the past, had been effectively eliminated.

The Achilles heel of Belgian policy, however, was their failure to interpret the political implications of the nationalism which was already sweeping across Africa. The Mission attached great importance to this lack of political foresight, which in the end came close to destroying all progress that the Belgians had tried so hard to establish, not only in the Trust Territory, but in the Congo as well. This concern was reflected extensively in its report on the political advancement of the Territory:

41

There is little doubt that the Administering Authority has introduced certain political reforms designed to develop Ruanda-Urundi toward its ultimate goal of self-government or independence. The Mission is concerned here primarily with the rate of that development, whether it is too rapid or too slow, how the present policy of the Administering Authority influences it and how soon the objective of self-government can be achieved without jeopardizing the stability of the state and its society. . . .

The Mission considers that a policy which does not pay equal attention to all fundamental human urges is unlikely to develop to the full the composite personality of the African . . . Moreover, in a feudal society such as exists in Ruanda-Urundi where economic security was traditionally guaranteed by the concentration of power in a few, it is particularly important that political education and development should be given a very high priority, for that is the only way of insuring the safe transition of a society from a feudal to a democratic form. Economic and social development alone cannot secure this end, for economic security and political stability are largely interdependent and one cannot exist for long without the other. Much of the economic good that may be achieved by the present policy will be nullified if the people's political growth fails to keep pace with economic development.

The Mission considers that urgent and serious attention should therefore be given to speeding up the political education of the people by granting them increasing doses of political power and responsibility and by other positive measures such as adult education, democratization of the indigenous authorities, adult suffrage, education for direct elections, etc. . . .

The Mission regrets its inability to agree with the views expressed by the Governor-General of the Belgian Congo. While no one can prophesy when a country will become ready for self-government or independence, it should be possible to estimate a period within which a people can be helped to develop in modern times with modern facilities toward this goal. The Mission does not believe that a prolonged period of tutelage covering three or four generations is necessary to achieve this objective. . . . The Mission's own impressions bear testimony to its faith in the innate qualities of the peoples of Ruanda-Urundi, and its belief that they too can [develop] to govern themselves in one generation.

It was at this point that Mr. Reid began to take issue with the other three of us. It was his judgment that the people, for the time being, would respond much more enthusiastically to a series of short-term programs rather than focusing on the politically provocative target of eventual independence. But I believe we all shared a sense of foreboding about the future of the Territory if reforms were not made in terms of colonial policy.

The next stop on the Mission's itinerary, after Ruanda-Urundi, was British-governed Tanganyika, the largest and most populous Trust Territory in Africa. Our planes landed in the town of Mwanza on the border of Lake Victoria, where we boarded a side-tracked private train which was to take us to Dar es Salaam after a few days of visiting in the Lake Province. Accommodations on the train were truly luxurious. Each member of the Mission, and the government officials who had been flown up from Dar es Salaam to be with us, were provided with a large private bedroom and bathtub.

The population of Tanganyika consisted of approximately eight million Africans and some 80,000 Arab and Asian traders who considered Tanganyika their home. Europeans numbered about 20,000, most of whom were professional people and government servants in the Territory on a temporary or transient basis. Only around 3,000 Europeans, consisting of farmers and their families, considered themselves as permanently settled in the country, so that the ratio of European settlers to Africans was on the minute scale of only one to about 25,000. This meant that settler problems over the long run would never become politically significant, as they had become in Kenya.

The administration of Tanganyika was headed by a Governor, who was responsible to the Colonial Office in London, but who in practice had unrestricted powers over all legislation and public policy. He was assisted by a Cabinet, an Executive Council and a Legislature, all of whose members he appointed. To make the Governor's control even tighter, each body was divided between Government officials and non-official members, the latter always being kept at least one vote in the minority.

The Government and the British Authorities had accepted the principle of parity of representation of the three despite the fact that Africans made up more than 90% of the vote, while the Asians and the Europeans consisted of less than 10%. As of 1955, each racial group was to have nine representatives. As before, all were to be appointed by the Governor, but for the first time they were to be chosen on a geographical basis: one person of each group from each of the eight Territorial Provinces and one from the capital of Dar es Salaam. To maintain the government's majority the number of official members was to be increased to twenty-eight and it was proposed that some of them should be persons holding quasi-official positions. The others should be non-officials, who would be required to promise to support the Government in all major policy matters.

The Lake Province was a favorable point of introduction to the Trust Territory, for here development was proceeding at an apparently greater rate than in the past in every field, and the beneficiaries were predominantly the Africans themselves.

The morning after the Mission's arrival at Mwanza, Rikhi Jaipal and I, accompanied by several British officials, motored out into the country to visit a native cotton cooperative where the African members were actually selling the cotton that they had raised.

While motoring along the dusty road on our way to the cooperative, we talked about the problem of cattle raids by the Masai with some frequency in this district.

The Masai, although few in number, are an extremely warlike tribe. There were only some 50,000 in Tanganyika and a similar number in adjoining Kenya. They are principally cattle people, who live mainly on blood and milk. In Tanganyika alone, they owned around 600,000 head of cattle, which were endlessly on the move from grazing area to water holes and back again. The younger boys' traditional duty is to watch over the herds and bring them back at night to Masai bomas, which are called *manyattas*, for milking and protection. The Masai people have persistently refused to change their way of life or to accept the methods of raising the standards of living which were being adopted by all the tribes around them. They live on the Masai steppes, an extensive flat and semi-arid area of land which stretches from the western part of Kenya across the Northern Province of Tanganyika.

What makes the Masai so feared is the standing army of fighters known as *moran*. The young Masai enter the warrior age grade at about eighteen years of age and remain as *moran* until they are around thirty. Their weaponry consists of long, heavy spears and tough cowhide shields. As part of the process of becoming a *moran*, each young man is expected either to kill a lion singlehanded or to kill a human being who is known to be an enemy of the tribe. When at war, in order to create a fierce appearance, they wear a lion's-mane headdress. Almost all of them have a handsome appearance and are distinguished from their elders by ocher-colored plaited hairdresses which are drawn down from the forehead to a point between the eyes.

While in service as *moran*, they have the time of their lives. For example, it is beneath their dignity to do manual labor of any kind. Their main purpose is to protect their own cattle and wherever possible to increase their wealth by raiding nearby tribes for their animals. Just as it was in the frontier days of the American West, cattle rustling is still an accepted form of business, not only in Africa, but wherever cattle-owning people live side by side.

Rikhi Jaipal and I, accompanied by a small party of British officials, then flew from Mwanza to Musoma. We were met at Musoma by the District Commissioner, the various chiefs of the area, and a large crowd of bystanders. We proceeded directly to the District Council Chambers, which was packed with people. From Musoma we motored to Zanaki, where we met another group of chiefs and a large crowd in the village Court House. Here we saw an actual trial taking place.

The next morning, we visited the leper settlement at Nkolandoto, which is run by some splendid American missionaries—mostly from Pennsylvania—who belonged to the African Inland Mission and, later, we went to the Williamson Diamond Mine near Shinyanga, one of the largest in Africa.

A few days after leaving Mwanza, our special train arrived at Tabora, where the Mission divided its work as there was so much to be seen and so little time to see it. I was invited to attend a secondary boy's school and another court which was in session. As we approached the building, we came upon a large crowd which was awaiting us. We sat down while red-turbaned warriors began to chant and dance. Next, the women started dancing and chanting and tapping a piece of metal which each one of them held in her hand.

After the dancing, we went into the open court house with the chief, followed by the warriors and the rest of the crowd. There, we were introduced to the official magistrate, who hears most of the cases coming before the court and to three elders who act as a jury. We stayed in court to hear two cases. The first was the case of two young men who had gone to a beer party, after which they had stolen three chickens from a third man. The next case was that of a young man who was accused of stealing 180 shillings from an old man who had put him up in his hut for the night.

When we left the court house, we were followed by the warriors who immediately asked if we would remain a while longer so that they could play their huge tribal drums, which were hung from a rope stretched between two poles. We were delighted to wait, so the drums began to boom and the warriors began to chant while the women chanted.

Later in the afternoon we motored to an Arab-type house where Stanley and Livingstone had lived for two months just after their famous meeting at nearby Ujiji on Lake Tanganyika.

On our way home we passed through the village where we had seen the dancing. The red-turbaned warriors were just breaking up, having divided an ox which the chief had slaughtered for them. I leaned out of the car window and waved. Responding to my gesture, one of the riflemen fired a musket shot into the air, a goodbye signal, marking the end of a warm and friendly day.

The next stop on the Mission's railroad journey came at Dodoma, the capital of the Central Province. The city lies astride the famous Cape-to-Cairo road running somewhat disjointedly from Capetown, South Africa, to Cairo, Egypt.

As our motor cars approached Mvumi, which lies on an open dusty plain, we saw in the distance that a great many people had collected to welcome us. There were hundreds and hundreds of them lined up on each side of the road for almost a mile. Upon our approach, the men began to clap and the women to make their shrill whoops. They were a fine-looking people, dressed much like the Masai. Like the Masai, the young warrior-type men of the Wagogo tribe braided their hair, which was held in place over the top of their heads by red clay.

When our cars had moved into the midst of the clapping, whooping throng, a young, very tall warrior jumped into the path of our car, leaping high in the air, time and again, bringing us to a stop. He then came around to the side of my car while I shoved out my hand to shake hands. This released us so that we could proceed again. Finally, we came to the chief's headquarters where we met Chief Mazengo, paramount chief of the Wagogo.

After the meeting we went out to watch the drumming and dancing which was going on everywhere. I then visited another group of dancers which was much smaller than the first. They were crowded around a drummer who sat on the ground beating a drum of substantial size. I was told later that the dances we saw were the dances held during the dry season. The dancing and chanting for the rainy season and the harvesting season are each quite different. Altogether, the hospitality which the Wagogo extended to us during the afternoon indicated the kind of spirit which bolsters a people preparing for eventual control of their own affairs.

It would be wrong to conclude that festivities dominated the travels of the United Nations Missions. To the contrary, the daily work of these Missions was taken up with endless inspections of schools, hospitals, tea and coffee estates; in fact economic education and social progress of all kinds. All of this work was necessary, but of itself did not provide much that would help the Mission to explore, or to react to African political thinking, which was to be the central emphasis of our homecoming report to the Trusteeship Council.

Before taking up the vital subject of Tanganyikan independence there is one aspect of the economic situation in Tanganyika which has not been touched upon. This concerned the extraordinary animal life to be found in East Africa, especially in Tanganyika. The Mission very kindly assigned Ian Berenson and me to undertake a quick survey of the situation, and we visited the Ngorongoro Crater, where the most spectacular display of animal life in Africa can be found. To get to the Crater, one's motor car has to wind slowly up an evermore tropical setting, until suddenly it arrives at the Crater's rim, where one suddenly comes upon a breathtaking view. You can see 2,000 feet below to the floor of the Crater volcano, some 100 square miles in extent. When examining the floor of the Crater through field glasses, you can see herd upon herd of wildebeest, zebra, gazelle, and here and there a rhino and perhaps a scarcely noticed pride of lions waiting to make a kill. The most facinating part of it all was the rough road cut along the top of the Crater rim. Travelling along this rough road one never knows what the bend in the next corner would reveal. More often than not, it would be a group of elephants busy with their interminable work of pulling up grass or pulling down tree branches. I remember rounding one curve and having to halt the car because of elephants crossing the rough roadway exactly opposite a huge, ugly-faced African buffalo, who was lying down chewing his cud. These buffalos are considered by many to be the most dangerous of African animals.

Berenson and I were invited to spend the night with Major Hewlett, Warden of the Park, whose house was several hundred yards to one side of the Crater road. He told us that one night a rhinoceros circled part of his house only to come face to face with a lion circling from the opposite direction. Both let out cries of surprise and ran away.

While many Africans at the time did not appreciate the

full value of their animal kingdom, it was more than apparent that in due course the animals would attract visitors from all over the world and would provide one of the most lucrative sources of government cash income.

Just beyond the Ngorongoro Crater stretched the huge Serengeti Plain which furnished the grazing land for literally hundreds of thousands of wildebeest and zebras. The result was that the Plain was inhabited by great numbers of lions. In fact, I was told that in the spring, when huge migrations of animals moved on to new feeding grounds, the roar of the accompanying lion predators was continuous.

So far I have dwelt upon the gayer and more pleasant side of African life and not upon the political side, which was to be the central theme of our Mission's report to the Trusteeship Council. By sheer coincidence, the Mission's visit occurred within a few weeks of the formation of the nationalistic Tanganyika African National Union (TANU), which was built upon the basis of the older Tanganyika African Association. TANU was headed by a brilliant schoolteacher, Julius Nyerere. It had already formed branches in various parts of the Trust Territory and was made to order for the nation to progress under the U.N. Charter toward independence. This pitted the brilliant personality of Nyerere against the empire-minded personality of Governor Twining, Governor of the Trust Territory.

By this time, it was becoming increasingly clear to me that our Chairman was basically pro-colonist. This presented me with an important opportunity, since it meant that on our four-man Mission I could, in good conscience, throw the influence of the United States with the anti-colonial representatives of India and El Salvador. This gave me an opportunity to counteract the Soviet accusations that the United States, in an endeavor not to offend its NATO colonial allies, was at heart, pro-colonial.

What astonished and infuriated the British, not only in Tanganyika but at home in the Colonial Office, was the report of the Mission that:

. . . . to give the territory—its government and its people together—a stronger sense of purpose, a more definite and better understood series of targets at which its successive political, economic and social development plans and programs could be aimed, would induce an atmosphere of understanding and confidence in which the country should be able to move more rapidly and smoothly ahead. The Mission believes that there is first of all a need for a more precise statement than appears yet to have been made, that a self-governing or independent Tanganyika will inevitably be a state primarily African in character with a government mainly in African hands.

. . . The Mission considers that there could be no more effective declaration of faith in the future of the Territory and its people than to fix the time within which they may be helped, with reasonable optimism as well as reasonable caution, to attain the goal. The Mission has already expressed its faith in the possibility of Ruanda-Urundi, a relatively less developed country, becoming self-governing in 20 to 25 years. Applying the same criteria and bearing in mind the striking development in Tanganyika during the last eight years, and despite its unevenness, the much larger areas of the territory and its widely dispersed population, the Mission believes that self-government is within reach of the people of Tanganyika much earlier. It must be borne in mind that other factors may well intervene, internally or from the outside, which will speed up the progress toward self-government. The point is that, even at the present pace of development, the people can be developed to become self-governing within a single generation.

In retrospect, few British people could conceive of Tanganyikan independence short of fifty or more years. The facts finally revealed that it became independent in seven years, with the full-fledged blessings of the Colonial Secretary and the Colonial Office.

Upon our arrival in Nairobi, Kenya, we had a conference with the Governor, Sir Edward Baring, the High Commission Administrator, and several others concerning the joint administrative arrangements between Tanganyika, Kenya and Uganda.

Shortly, accompanied by a Mr. Kerr, a member of the High Commission, we struck out for the famous White Highlands, an area in dispute between the Africans and the British. The countryside was absolutely beautiful, rolling hills covered thickly with green trees and huge cultivated areas of coffee, maize, and banana trees. Part of it was for Europeans and one could see many big white houses. Part of it was for what was termed the "native reserves," where the Africans lived and cultivated their section of the land. The road led continuously from European to African and African to European areas.

We saw many people travelling on foot by the sides of the road and most of them were members of the huge Kikuyu tribe, which consists of approximately 2 million people.

At lunch at the hotel, we noted that all the young European men were carrying revolvers and our friend, Mr. Kerr, said that he would have carried along his revolver, too, if he would have known beforehand that he would be asked to accompany us. A few weeks before our arrival, the cook in his house had been cut to pieces by Mau Mau terrorists. The worst of it was that the Mau Mau terrorists had been led to his house by his most trusted African servant, who had been with him for years.

It is hard to understand how Europeans could bear living in such an atmosphere of terrorism. But every family that packed up to go home played right into the hands of the Mau Mau and would make it so much the worse for those families that remained.

On our way home after lunch, we stopped on the top of a hill where a Kikuyu Home Guard lookout post had been constructed. I found it to be a most amazing structure. It consisted of a wooden stockade with a tin roof, out of which arose a lookout tower about 50-60 feet high. Surrounding the stockade was a moat about five feet in depth,into the sides of which were dug long, sharp bamboo spikes. Leading into the stockade was a drawbridge which could be lifted up into the air at night so that there would be no entrance to the fortification whatever.

The so-called Mau Mau revolt was an insurrection caused by misunderstandings over lands, tribal customs, and very poor race relations. Being a secret terrorist operation, it was difficult to know where and when Mau Mau would break out. That is why we saw so many soldiers and armed civilians on the streets of Nairobi.

In the city of Nairobi, the military atmosphere was striking. Almost every European carried a submachine gun or a revolver. In one case, I noticed a young woman carrying her purse in one hand and a rifle in the other.

Two or three days were sufficient for us to complete our work in Nairobi, after which we were scheduled to take an Italian plane to Somalia.

When we arrived at Nairobi's East Airport to take the special military plane which the Italian Government had provided to fly us to Mogasdiscio, the plane was not quite ready, so we had some time to observe the military operations at the airport.

This airport was the base for all the Royal Air Force planes operating against the Mau Mau. The place was filled with great four-engined Lincoln bombers, light observation bombers, small police spotter planes and jet aircraft.

Finally, our plane took off and in half an hour we were flying in the completely new and different world of Italian Somalia.

Governor Martino, Mr. Spinelli, the Italian Representative on the Trusteeship Council, and other high officials were standing by the plane as we debarked in Mogadiscio. There was a guard of honor and a military band; also delegations representing the main political parties of Somalia. We then climbed into a number of cars and were escorted by white-uniformed motorcycle police through the city, which is entirely Arabian and Moorish in design. There were many trees and I found the place to have great charm and beauty.

We had an enormous, French-type lunch at the Governor's House and after lunch we were taken to the special guest house, near the Governor's House, where the light-blue U.N. flag floated over the roof of our bright white building. We were surrounded outside by trees and flower gardens.

The next day, we paid an official visit to the Territorial Council, which was in session in Mogadiscio.

Mogadiscio is closely bordered by the sea, sand dunes, the desert and semi-arid wastes. First built in 900 A.D., it stretches over a very shallow depression a few hundred feet below the white wall of the Government House area. The main part of the city consisted of scattered one- and two-story structures, in between which were a number of Somali *bomas*. These *bomas* were made of low thornbush reeds.

Mogadiscio is like a North African city—pure white for the most part—with many small mosques. It is a very cheerful, sunny city bang up against a straight seacoast, protected only by a series of long breakwaters. One big, white liner was lying off shore.

Some of the women wore white or colored veils over their faces, but most were more emancipated and wore brilliantly colored clothing. All these people were city people and not at all representative of most of the population of Somalia, which is Nomadic.

During the morning, the Mission again visited the Territorial Council, which had assembled to address a number of speeches to us describing the outstanding Somali problems. While listening to them, I noticed that the back of the chamber, stretching from side to side, was a line of huge, blown-up photos. To my astonishment, my own very bald head seemed to dominate at least a half-dozen! These photos were the ones taken on the arrival of the Mission at Mogadiscio and at the time of our first visit to the Territorial Council, which was soon to become the first elected Somali Assembly.

I later persuaded John Reid to come with me to see some of the sights in this really fascinating city. First, we went to the marketplace or, rather, a long market or shopping street. Nowhere in Africa, except possibly at Fort Archambault in French Equatorial Africa, had I seen anything to beat the color or interesting atmosphere of this part of Mogadiscio. It was definitely cleaner than anything I had seen in the Far East of in other parts of Africa, except in certain parts of the Hausa country in West Africa.

Then we went to the semi-nomad part of the city, which I observed through my binoculars each morning before breakfast.

Overall, I was exhausted, politically, by the Somalis. While they are among the most personally attractive people I have ever seen, they can "do in" even the patient listener when it comes to listening to their political and economic complaints.

The next day, we flew to Chisimaio, where we were met by the chief Italian officials and many other people. Then we visited a school and our presence turned it into a big day for the children. They were quite enchanting marching around, singing a song, giving us presents, and performing a special calisthenics drill to the accompaniment of whistled orders.

Later came an ordeal. We drove to a main office building in town to hear the citizens' petitions and complaints, but to our horror the street and square were crowded with excitable Somalis, hundreds and hundreds of them.

We were led into the "hearing room" while the crowds began to shout and jostle in their attempt to follow us in. It was frightening and I was worried that a full-scale riot might develop. All afternoon we heard one protesting group after another, including a group of women who wanted the right to vote. When the labor committee came in to see us, a large crowd collected just outside the windows and became so obstreperous at one point that a stone came through one of the windows, aimed at one of the unhappy Somali policemen. Their own leaders kept leaning out the windows of our hearing room, telling them that they had gotten a fair hearing from us and should disperse.

Finally, we were free to visit the Juba River, which is a broad, muddy stream, bordered by tall, luxuriant green trees and heavy undergrowth. It provides the only cultivatable land in Somalia, except for the Webbi Scebeli. This cultivatable land only extends out from the river about half a mile, or a mile at the most. Bordering the river are large Italian farms which were taken from the Somalis in the 1930's, and which were causing the same kind of trouble that the White Highlands were causing in Kenya. We had complaint after complaint about them from the Somalis who lived next door but couldn't get enough water because the European farms were interposed between them and the river.

We crossed the river on a cable ferry, manned by 25 Somali cable haulers. While they were hauling at the cables they would sing a regular chant. The songmaster would do the "thinking" part of the verses supported by the rest of the crew, who sang the refrain. It was like any seagoing chantey, except that they added the usual African rhythmic touch. This they supplied by stamping their feet in time to the song. When we went over on the ferry they were singing songs about their own lives. When we came back in the afternoon they sang some songs about us.

Our next destination was Bardera, far up the Juba River. We followed the course of the river generally and made side excursions over the arid country below. This flight also gave us a good idea of how much river-bordering land had been "alienated" or handed over to the Europeans for the cultivation of their large farms which blanketed off the Somalis from the available river-front land.

On landing at Bardera we were met by the district officials and a guard of honor. The town of Bardera was a very hot, but most attractive, community of neatly laid out and walled-in huts. Large groups of people were lined up and clapped as we motored by. Our first duty upon arrival at the Resident's house was the difficult job of listening to committee after committee of earnest Somalis who wanted to tell us of all the problems they were up against. Their stories were all the same; no water and border clashes with Ethiopians. The borderline between Ethiopia and Somalia was—and still is—in dispute.

After lunch we flew from Bardera to Baidoa, an interior city in Somalia. The land below was almost barren and literally speckled with low thornbushes and dwarf acacia trees. Some of the soil was almost crimson red. We saw flocks and flocks of goats, all dashing madly about at the noise of the plane overhead although the camels never seemed to mind the plane.

When we arrived at Baidoa, which was cooler, being

on a small plateau 1,000 feet above the plain, we were met by troops and a huge double-line of Somalis, accompanied by a goodly sprinkling of small boys, who wanted to be in on everything. There must have been several hundred people there.

As soon as we were installed, I asked for a jeep and was driven slowly through the town and the market, one of the biggest in Somalia. My guide was a Mr. Gaspari, the economic head for the Government, who drove me around Baidoa in a government jeep during the morning and much of the afternoon. First we saw one of the recently-completed U.S.-Italian-built wells run by a windmill, with a gasoline pump to supply power when the wind fails.

The marketplace was filled with people, including large numbers of the nomads clad in light brown camel cloths and enormous fuzzy haircuts. I saw the place where the camels were waiting to be loaded, and another place where camels were being sold. Everywhere we went we were surrounded quickly by a large crowd of men and boys.

From the marketplace we started on our drive to Uegit, where there were a number of wells that I particularly wanted to see. We drove mile after mile of straight dirt road through endless Somali thornbush country. How anybody could survive on this land I could not understand. We stopped at one point to see a *uar*, a large catch basin for rainwater. This one was dry and the semi-nomads of the nearby village were waiting for the rain which a cloudy sky indicated would soon commence. The young men of this village had been forced to depart with the cattle, camels and goats due to lack of water. It was a terrible life that these water shortages imposed on these people. The Italians were about to start on a *uar* construction program which called for 260 *uar* within two years. Each *uar* would provide, during the dry season, enough stored-up water from the rainy season to meet the wants of 10 families and their animals—or 2,600 families in all. It was calculated that this program would tend to eliminate the necessity of roaming around the country in search of water. In other words, it created small permanent villages, around which could be constructed schools, dispensaries, etc.

When we finally got to Uegit—which was a very small

village outside an old white Italian fort, I saw a sight I will never forget. There were hundreds of camels grouped around a well, with herds of other camels a few hundred yards away, awaiting their turn for water. There were also great quantities of goats, but goats and cattle have to give way to camels, who have drinking priority as they have traveled much farther distances. The well itself was a large circular affair, perhaps 20 feet in diameter and 30 feet deep. The water in it was very low, but at the rim of the well the nomad herdsmen were throwing bucket after bucket into the water which were then hauled up by ropes. They would dump the contents into troughs which sloped off into a large circular trough, from which the camels were drinking. The whole scene demonstrated more dramatically than anything else could, the terrible water shortage of Somalia, and showed how hard feelings could be aroused between the tribes in disputes over water rights at the wells.

From here we motored up to the village of Uegit, outside of which was drawn up a long line of Somali men and women. It was impossible to shake hands with everyone, but I did go down the line, sort of like Ike or Teddy Roosevelt, with my hand high in the air, waving and shouting *Salaam*. I was given a few petitions, and then responded with a short statement regarding the water wells and the boundary problems. After this I waved goodbye to the accompaniment of more clapping and whoops as we drove off to inspect the police force.

In the evening, the Italian Provincial Commissioner held a reception for Rikhi Jaipal and myself, to which the local chiefs, Muslim notables, political party leaders and Italian officials were invited.

As we came upon the town of Dinsor we saw the usual long lines of people waiting for us. The two main political parties were lined up, with their political flag carried by someone in the center. There were also holy men, notables and chiefs. Some were dressed in the most brilliant blues and reds with gold embroidery. As we passed by their lines, they gave us the usual treatment of clapping and whooping.

Dinsor was remarkable for its natural wells, and there

were easily 15 large shallow wells, 20 feet deep, and small-bore wells, 18 inches in diameter, sunk deep into the ground. Every well was being worked by two or more Somalis, who would throw buckets down into the water below and then haul them up to the surface. Sometimes they would do it to the accompaniment of a song. One of the songs I heard was said to be a song for the cows. It could be seen that the poor cows were very thirsty from the way they would plunge their mouths into the water tub each time it was filled from a supply coming up from the well.

All the wells in Dinsor were dug and privately owned by individual families. The water was used for the family and its livestock and was also sold to nomad customers coming in from the distance. At the end of the day's work, each well was covered over with sticks and, during the night, a guard slept nearby.

Water certainly was the whole story in Somaliland, but one had to see the wells in operation to sense how intensely true this was. I was told that one out of each seven years was a drought year, when the rains did not live up to expectation. When this happened, the tribes in this area had to move their animals over to the Webbi-Scebelli River, where their presence was most unpopular and caused tribal fighting.

We left Baidoa early by motor cars for Bur Acaba, where there were scores and scores of petitioners waiting to talk to us, but Rikhi Jaipal made an excellent speech which seemed to satisfy the crowd.

A little way out of Uanle Uen we got an idea of how feverish this business of watering animals can get. We came to a place where there was nearly a thousand head of cattle collected in herds, standing around waiting for their turn to drink in a muddy pool of water. The newly-drilled well was still being test-pumped. The animals were collected in less than two acres of space and the air was filled with dust from their never-ceasing movements.

In the middle of it all was the muddy pool, divided by mud walls into three connecting sections. In each section stood two or three bareheaded, mud-spattered Somalis, armed with sticks, standing knee deep in water facing a line of perhaps a dozen cattle, who were drinking water without pause. The cattle were kept rigidly in place with their feet out of the water so as not to make it any muddier than it was. Whenever a thirsty animal from a strange herd, not entitled to drink at this time, tried to wedge its way into the drinking line, it was prodded out by the men's sticks, so violently that it would run away. The whole atmosphere was overpowered by the feeling of thirst.

The men were so intense, even hectic, in the way they controlled the animals and protected their drinking process that it was easy to visualize how quickly a dispute over who could have a turn to drink next might arise. This scene, more than anything I had previously observed, represented the atmosphere and spirit of this very poor and parched country. Before this well began delivering water, the animals here had to go some 20 or 30 miles away for their supply.

The Mission spent another day interviewing Somali petitioners. One man said he didn't believe anything said to him by the Italian Government, or the U.N. Then he raised his shirt and showed us a scar from a stab wound in the back, and said, "Long live Pandit Nehru."

Another very interesting day followed. Rikhi Jaipal and I and an interpreter flew from Mogadiscio to Belet Uen, in the interior. Belet Uen is a frontier town, from which we motored up to the actual border of Ethiopia, at a place called Fer Fer. We wanted to get first-hand information on the number one political problem of Somalia, its border with Ethiopia.

On our arrival at the Belet Uen airstrip, which was just a marked area in the middle of a sandy plain, we were met by the provincial commissioner who, after a few short formalities, drove us up in a couple of jeeps to Fer Fer, about 30 miles distant.

The countryside around Fer Fer was extremely barren. Each side of the border was simply marked by two guard posts, which were mud huts, and a gate, blocking the road. Not more than 20 yards separated the two posts. A little way off were two very small villages, each occupied by Somalis who have been divided by the arbitrary borderline. In the distance and to one side was a truly picturesque Ethiopian fort, with battlements and lookout stations surrounded by barbed wire.

We walked up to the barrier on the Italian side and soon there was a crowd of Somalis lined up behind the gate from the Ethiopian side. We had a long and most interesting conversation with them. The chief spokesman, aged about 35, explained that his father, according to Muslim law, had four wives, two living on the Ethiopian side and two on the Somali side. There are many similar cases of family split-ups because of the arbitrary borderline. The thing that irritated the Somalis the most was the looting problem. Somalis from the Ethiopian side were continually crossing over to the Somali side to steal cattle and other animals from their brothers. If they were not caught by the Italian-controlled Somali police, they could get away with their loot, because there was no law and order on the Ethiopian side. But, if the Somalis on the Italian side under U.N. Trusteeship tried to retaliate and recover their losses in kind, they were stopped short by the Italian-controlled border police.

This looting was a daily threat. Ten days before our visit there had been a serious and successful raid. In this case, however, when the raiders retired across the border with their loot, the Ethiopian soldiers from the fort swiped the cattle from the raiders and were eating the animals as part of their daily ration.

After our visit to the border we returned to Belet Uen, where we interviewed some 30 or 40 refugees from the Ethiopian side. These men were mostly former chiefs, shopkeepers, one Sultan, some elders and notables. In fact, almost all of them had left the Ethiopian side in order to protest to the U.N. through our Mission.

Belet Uen itself was a very attractive-looking town. Much of it was sprawled out under groves of tall multi-trunk palm trees. These palm trees were unlike anything I had ever seen before. At this point, the muddy Webbi Scebelli River, which was quite wide, wound through the settlement. On the outskirts beyond the tree areas were many hundreds of thatched houses surrounded by stick stockades, through which ran broad streets crossed by narrow lanes. Beyond the houses or huts were miles of wind-eroded, yellow, sandy plains.

The Provincial Commissioner, at my request, took us around the town in his jeep. Several times we saw groups of nomads sitting down and resting near their kneeling camels.

The next day, we had a long, final business meeting with the Governor and some of his subordinates. From there we drove to the Airport to meet the plane which was to fly us to Cairo the following day. It brought in three high Italian officials—a cabinet minister, a Senator and the Chairman of the Foreign Relations Committee of the Italian lower House. Many Somalis and almost all of the Italian officials of Mogadiscio were on hand to meet them. They came because the next day was Flag Day, when the Somalis were to put their new flag into commission.

Flag Day was our last day in Somalia and it was a truly historic occasion. The flag is light blue with a five-pointed white star in the middle. These five points stood for Somalia itself; for British and French Somaliland; for the Ogaden, across the border in Ethiopia; and for the northern part of Kenya on the southern border. All of these together were considered to be greater Somalia which, it was hoped, would become united one day.

There were literally thousands of Somalis crowded into the Square in front of the Administration Building, where the flag-raising ceremonies took place. People were everywhere, including roof tops, and children were singing. Promptly at 9 a.m. we all went out onto the balcony high above the Square, where the Governor led off the speakers. When he finished, he said, "Viva Somali," at which time there was cheering and whooping from the crowds. Then John Reid spoke, and after him came two of the special Italian visiting officials from Rome. Then, Abdi Nur and Aden Abdulla, Vice Presidents of the Territorial Council, and leaders of the two chief political parties—the Hisbia Digil Mirfle and Somali Youth League—both spoke. Finally, the meeting was blessed by the senior Qadi, who is the most learned Somali in matters of Islamic law. He was dressed in a beautiful dark blue, silk robe with gold-red trimmings. The words, which were a sort of prayer, were punctuated by frequent Muslim "Amens" from the crowd. Then the blue flag with its white star was raised on its mast and the crowd let loose with shouting and clapping while three airplanes made a series of swoops overhead, dropping great quantities of paper Somali flags. It was a sight I never forgot.

After that the crowds wandered through the streets singing the Somali anthem. On our way back to our headquarters, it seemed as if every single building in the city was flying the new flag.

Later in the afternoon, Aden Abdulla, who was destined to become the first Prime Minister of Somalia, and Abdi Nur were kind enough to take me around the city. We visited the political headquarters of the four biggest parties which were holding patriotic rallies out of respect for the new flag.

We first visited the headquarters of the Somali Youth League. This organization, which was led by Abdulla, was by far the largest and most influential political party in Somalia. When we arrived a big crowd had begun to collect. The women were assembled in a walled-in courtyard. Adjoining this was a very large hall where the men were asembling. As we were to return later on we only stayed for a moment and then proceeded to the headquarters of Hisbia Digil Mirfle, the President of which was Abdi Nur. Here we entered another big courtyard, which was already well filled with people. The women were out in the open and the men seated under a covered area.

We were led onto a platform at one end, where we sat down on chairs behind a table on which were three or four hand microphones. The crowd was addressed by Abdi Nur, then I was asked to speak. I spoke one sentence at a time through an interpreter, and after each interpretation the crowd would clap. When we left through lanes of people there was much clapping and whooping. I had to keep waving and smiling as we walked along. I felt a little strange as this was an unusual role for me.

Next we visited the headquarters of another party, the Party Democratico Somalia. I met the President and officers, who showed us their offices. They then took us out into an open courtyard which was crowded with hundreds of men and women. I was led through the crowd up onto the platform. Many of the older men, sitting in the front row of the audience, got up and saluted as we passed. On the platform there was a flourish of bugling as we walked to our seats. Here again I had to make a short speech. I started out by bringing them the greetings of the U.N. and then the United States. I told them that our Mission had been well received by the people and that we were going to do our best to help them. Then, after congratulating them on their new flag, I said, "Long live Somalia"— which seemed to go over well with the crowd, judging by their animated reaction.

We then returned to the Somali Youth League hall, which was packed with men. They opened up a lane about two feet wide through which we were led to a small table at the end of the hall. As soon as we sat down a young man with a fez on his head began singing a song to the accompaniment of drums and a small portable piano. He sang a number of verses, after which came the speechmaking, during which both Abdi Nur and Aden Abdulla spoke at length about the help already given to Somalia by the United States and their hope that it would continue in the future. In fact, Abdulla said that he considered the United States more important to the future of Somalia than the U.N. The feeling on the subject of American aid worried me as I feared they were counting too heavily on the U.S. to bail them out if they got into financial trouble.

From nine o'clock to two in the morning, the Italians held a huge garden party. From the party we went directly to the airport, where we said good-bye to countless friends and took off for Cairo in the middle of the night.

Chapter V

The Report Imbroglio

Our Mission's report raised a furious storm in Tanganyika, where British officialdom and businessmen alike directed a stream of criticism, much of it at me. Even the British Colonial Office in London sent a protest to their representatives at the U.N. Among many criticisms, they insisted that the report contained 125 inaccuracies. The majority of these were so insignificant as to be picayune. In fact, they were little more than the protest of the Colonial Office, which abandoned its usual dignity and clearheadedness. This was most surprising as the British seldom lost their calm or acted in an undignified manner.

In the meantime, my greatest fear was that our Chairman, John Reid, might desire to present a unanimous report and therefore change his pro-colonial vote. This was of real concern to me since I believed that unless there was major dissent within the Mission, the statements about conditions in Tanganyika which I wanted emphasized would lose their impact. Under these circumstances it was not surprising that I became worried when John Reid asked me to have a private conference with him. During this conference I was delighted to have him ask me, "What do you think Sir Alan Burns [the British representative] will think about the report?" This gave me a perfect opportunity to explain to Mr. Reid that I represented the United States and not the British government, and John indicated that he appreciated my position.

Thus far, everything had proceeded just as I had hoped and, since the subject concerned a specific contribution by the United States to the U.N., I felt on firm grounds. I was quite pleased until Ambassador Lodge received a letter from Secretary Dulles. Dulles asserted that:

> We are confronted by the problem of determining the United States position in regard to certain parts of the Reports of the Trusteeship Council's 1954 Visiting Mission of the Trust Territories of Tanganyika. These Reports are permeated with the principle of establishing hypothetical time limits for the attainment of various stages of self-government.
>
> In the past the United States, as a general rule, has not supported the establishment of time-tables for the achievement of self-government, and is unwilling to do so in the present instances. Our immediate problem arises from the fact that the United States Representative in the Trusteeship Council and member of the four-man Visiting Mission to the East African Trust Territories, Mr. Mason Sears, has endorsed the three Reports without reservation.
>
> As a member of the Visiting Mission which operated as an agency of the United Nations, Mr. Sears served in his individual capacity. Therefore, the question of his right to express his own views is not an issue, nor does the Department fail to recognize in this situation that there is ample room for honest differences among individuals. On the other hand, all members of the Visiting Mission are officials of their respective Governments and nominated by them. As such it might be expected in some quarters that they would reflect their Government's views.
>
> Our general policy in the colonial field was restated by me before the CIO Convention in Cleveland on November 18, 1953, when I said that the orderly translation from colonial to self-governing status should be carried resolutely to a completion [but that] the development of genuine independence is a task of infinite difficulty and delicacy, [and] zeal needs to be balanced by patience. This basis for our policy regarding trust and

other non-self-governing territories has been stated repeatedly by United States spokesmen including Mrs. Frances P. Bolton and Mr. O.D. Jackson at the Eighth and Ninth General Assemblies, respectively. . . .

[Omitted here is the still-classified paragraph ordering me to inform the Trusteeship Council that my views as presented in the Visiting Mission's Report, were in disagreement with U.S. Policy, and therefore I was to repudiate the stand that I had taken on the floor of the Trusteeship Council.]

You are aware of the frequent need we have to rely upon our friends in the United Nations for support in obtaining positions to which we attach importance. This, however, is not the sole reason why we must not alienate unnecessarily our NATO allies and some of our staunchest supporters in the United Nations. We have problems of our own in the dependent areas field regarding which we require the sympathetic understanding and support of the largest possible majority of United Nations Members. For example, if we should endorse a general 20-25 year timetable for the attainment of self-government in Ruanda-Urundi or Tanganyika, the Belgians, British, or any other United Nations Member, could argue cogently that self-government for the widely scattered islands of our Trust Territory should be envisaged in a much shorter time because their peoples generally are more advanced, and have had considerable experience through contacts with the outside world. This could be quite embarrassing for us since we are on record against the establishment of a timetable for the Trust Territory of the Pacific Islands. As recently as the Fourteenth Session of the Trusteeship Council, High Commissioner Midkiff stressed the importance we attach to the principle of not imposing an arbitrary rate of development. It is precisely because we attach importance to the sound development of self-government that our policy emphasizes economic, social and educational advancement, a policy which finds full expression in the trusteeship provisions of the Charter. Thus in the Trusteeship Council and Committees of the General Assembly we should continue to stress balanced developments leading to effective and enduring self-government rather than giving the impression that we

favor a hasty imposition of "western" political patterns.
        I appreciate how carefully you have striven to maintain the delicate balance that is incumbent upon us in the United Nations activities regarding dependent area matters which have occupied the attention of political committees in recent General Assemblies. In the Trusteeship Council and elsewhere in the United Nations we certainly do not wish to impair our independent position by aligning ourselves automatically with other administering powers or allowing them to think that they can always count on our support. It is, however, reasonable for them to want to know where we stand and whether we have changed our position.
        The 1954 Visiting Mission's Reports are regarded by various Offices in the Government where they have been studied as unnecessarily controversial and tendentious. It is felt that criticisms of administrations are not balanced by a proper amount of credit for accomplishments and appreciation of the magnitude of the problems. The Department, after consultations with the Departments of Interior, Defense and the Navy, believes that the United States Representative in the Trusteeship Council cannot support action which would endorse the principle of establishing hypothetical timetables. In case the Council is asked to endorse other conclusions contained in these Reports, the United States Representative should use as guides our past positions and general statements to which I have referred along with the current position papers.
        I am sure that you share our appreciation of the gravity of colonial problems wherever they arise in the United Nations, and our need to speak with one voice in regard to them, particularly in view of the tight-rope we are continually obliged to walk in relation to those matters.

        As a result of this letter, I was required to repudiate my stand on the floor of the Trusteeship Council in a session where speech after speech was being made by the nation's administering Trust Territories that were vitriolic in their criticism of me. The unhappy result was that among the Africans in Africa, I received considerable credit for my stand but failed completely in my goal, which was to obtain credit for the United States. I felt that I was fully justified in attempting to achieve this goal by supporting the principle of target dates since, contrary to what Mr. Dulles stated in the second paragraph of his letter, U.S. policy since the Roosevelt administration had supported target dates—both in principle and in fact.

The nature of the Council's opposition to the Mission's report was such that TANU decided to send Julius Nyerere himself to the Trusteeship Council in order to explain the Mission's findings. In defending the Mission's report, he explained to the Council that:

> Tanganyika as a candidate for nationhood had three distinct advantages over many of its neighbors. It had a large number of tribes of which none was dominant, thus it was spared strife from breaking out between two or three large rival tribes. Since Tanganyika, during the time it was a trusteeship territory, had been neglected by the British, in favor of the crown colony of Kenya and its prosperous white highlands, Tanganyika had only a small community of white settlers to resist the rise of African nationalism.

Nyerere explained to the Council that Tanganyikans wanted independence and with independence in mind, he and his colleagues on July 7, 1954, officially reorganized the already established Tanganyika African Association as the Tanganyika National African Union (TANU). He also indicated that he had been unanimously elected as its President.

Governor Twining's response to the TANU's dispatch of Nyerere to New York was straightforward and predictable. He sent his own three-man delegation to support the government's position in direct opposition to Nyerere. He also urged Father Walsh to refuse to allow Nyerere to be absent from teaching his classes, implying that Nyerere's political activities verged on sedition. To his credit, Walsh refused, asking, "If it's sedition, why isn't Nyerere in jail?"

Perhaps the most outrageous thing of all occurred when the British government persuaded the American government to confine Nyerere's movements to a few blocks within the physical vicinity of the U.N. itself and limited his stay to twenty-four hours. One can hardly imagine the lack of sensitivity and even stupidity of the British government in making such an outrageous request of one who subsequently became one of the leading statesmen of the African continent. And one can certainly question the wisdom of American decision-makers in acquiescing to their folly.

The reaction of the United States government was a severe blow to me as I had thought that I had finally found a formula which could be supported by the U.S. without upsetting any of Mr. Dulles' cold-war policies and his subsequent attachment to the demands of our NATO allies.

Before ending this account of the dilemma which faced so many of us, it should be noted that at this time Stalin and the USSR were seen as a military threat to our interests everywhere in the world. Somehow, it was felt that if he could subvert Africa, he could outflank the West and become the dominant force throughout the world. In fact, in a contemporary development, while the climactic battle of Dien Bien Phu was in progress, Secretary Dulles and Vice President Nixon went to Eisenhower, suggesting that we supply American aid to the French. Fortunately, they were promptly and decisively turned down by the President.

The policy of Mr. Dulles and the State Department was best exemplified in the clarification I was obliged to give on the issue on the floor of the Trusteeship Council in response to the letter from Dulles concerning target dates. This clarification stated that as a member of the Visiting Mission I had taken a view which differed to some extent from that of my government.

While recognizing the merit of target dates for self-government in cases where the territory concerned was close to the attainment of that status, the U.S., according to Mr. Dulles, considered a timetable too rigid to be useful in the case of Tanganyika. This policy was adhered to in the belief that in some instances, self-government could be achieved sooner than the target dates set in a timetable, and that therefore it would be difficult to estimate progress. For these reasons, the U.S. would not support the timetable principle for Tanganyika. This was done despite the fact that we had set an independence date for the Philippines in 1934. Ironically, it should be noted that the British government ultimately resorted to the use of exactly such designated target dates.

During the seven years that I represented the U.S. on the Trusteeship Council, I never ceased to be disturbed at having to describe an American policy as trying to be all things to all men. As a newcomer to the government and ignorant about U.N. and State Department policies, I found it disturbing and frustrating to learn that, for Cold War reasons, the U.S. had abandoned its traditional role as champion of "self-determination" in order not to offend the colonial interests in Africa of our NATO allies in Europe.

To be on the side of European colonialism seemed to me totally unnatural to the U.S., where public opinion had rightly been long-conditioned by the background of our own war for independence and the subsequent anti-colonial instincts of our people. It is well to remember the anti-colonialism which was already developing among the increasingly influential forces of liberalism throughout Europe and which had long inflamed the millions in Asia and Africa. To run contrary to this preponderant world-wide feeling seemed to me as if the American people were being unnecessarily obliged to swallow a natural pride in our past in order to protect ourselves from some highly debatable danger from the Soviet Union throughout the world in the present. For the U.S. to back down from its traditional sympathy toward people struggling for self-determination took all the uplift, all of the idealism, out of our foreign policy. To most of the world it was an unanticipated and totally unnecessary buckling-under to the colonial interests of Europe. It made our government look like a conspirator on the side of Imperialism instead of as a champion of independence.

The reasons for such an about-face in U.S. policy were summed up by Mr. Dulles in one of his early speeches as Secretary of State. In this speech, which was delivered before the 1953 Convention of the C.I.O., he declared that the danger of Soviet aggressiveness was a "good and sufficient reason why the U.S. should show unity with its Western Allies," both in and out of the U.N. In words with particular applicability to Africa, the Secretary pointed out that:

> The Soviet leaders in mapping their strategy for world conquest, hit on nationalism as a device for absorbing the colonial peoples. Stalin, in his classic lecture on the Foundations of Leninism, says that "the road to victory of the revolution in the West lies through the revolutionary alliance with the liberation movement of the colonies and independent countries." There is then outlined a two-phased—and two-faced—program. In the first place the Communist agitators were to whip up the nationalistic aspirations of the people so that they will rebel violently against the existing order. Then, before newly won independence can become consolidated and vigorous in its own right, Communists will take over the new government and use this power to "amalgamate" the peoples into the Soviet orbit.

It was clear from this highly emotional statement that Mr. Dulles feared that Stalin's strategy might succeed, that the African masses could be manipulated by the Russians, and that Africa could become a continent from which international communism could outflank the Atlantic Community. This was a reaction which seriously misjudged the vitality of African nationalism and the influence of its leaders. It also appeared to involve a judgment that the best way to block communist-inspired violence and political domination in Africa was to support the continuance of colonial controls until such time as the territories concerned were considered ready by white standards to assume some form of self-government, presumably allied to the European Empires. To the European governments in the early 1950's, this often meant the prolongation of colonial relationships until some vague date in the future, say fifty or even one hundred years away.

I had great respect for the devoted services which Mr. Dulles gave to our country, he traveled so much and was so preoccupied with negotiating regional treaties to contain the spread of communism all over the world, that the time remaining to him was insufficient to give him adequate opportunity to consider the conditions governing African-American relations. At the same time, it is only fair to say that Mr. Dulles himself, seemed to be dissatisfied with the way his policies were being received. This was apparent in the spring of 1953 when, following his journey to South Asia and the North East, he openly recognized that U.S. colonial policy had become "unnecessarily ambiguous" and that "without breaking from the framework of western unity, we can pursue our traditional dedication to political liberty" and that "in reality, the Western powers can gain rather than lose from an orderly development of self-government." Nothing was ever done to make this more than a philosophic observation. A few weeks later, on Jan. 12, 1954, the Secretary made another speech in which he declared that:

> We intend that our nation shall continue showing its historic mission of how good can be the fruits of freedom. That policy carries with it the need to abstain from diplomatic moves which would seem to endorse captivity. Otherwise we would in effect be conspiring against freedom. I can assure you that we shall never seek illusory security for ourselves by such a "deal".

But such a "deal" between ourselves and the Colonial Empires was exactly what most of the world thought we were engaging in. We cannot escape the fact that it was a deal very much at the expense of Africa. Like the old saw about which comes first, the chicken or the egg, in this case it was about freedom or the containment of Russia. Accordingly, Mr. Dulles' eloquent words and sincere feelings about "freedom" could not be translated into action without restricting his policy of containment. This obviously pointed up the dilemma which was clearly disturbing to him and from which he and his principal advisors in the State Department never succeeded in extricating themselves.

Altogether, this was a critical time for Mr. Dulles. He was subjected to the strongest kind of pressures both at home and abroad. At home, Senator Joseph McCarthy of Wisconsin was still an insidious, much-feared factor in the political life of the U.S. Many people, in and out of public office, were still being branded communist sympathisers, disloyal to the U.S. The Secretary had inherited a State Department whose morale had been very seriously damaged by the unfounded accusations of the Senator. Public concern in the U.S. over Russian communism was riding high and was unnecessarily exaggerated even in the opinion of our European associates.

There was also the influence exercised by the military-industrial complex which President Eisenhower was later to warn against. Under the influence of a military psychology, which produced our enormous capacity for nuclear overkill, Africa was primarily a continent in which the Pentagon could plan for a grand defense in even greater depth. Because of their professional training and responsibilities, it would be unrealistic to expect the defense planners to do other than to encourage any move or any policy of the State Department which they believed would increase the value of their military interests in Africa.

Finally, there were pressures from the colonial offices in Europe and especially the white-settler groups in Africa which were exceedingly hostile toward the U.S. because of what they perceived to be the American public's bias against colonialism. Out of these influences and others came an operating policy toward Africa which seemed to many people to be fundamentally unsound in conception, self-defeating in practice, and damaging to the influence and reputation of the U.S. with the leaders and moulders of public opinion throughout the African and Asian worlds, the very people with whom we would be dealing in the 1970's and 1980's.

It was hard to accept the accuracy of the basic premise which suggested to the Africans that it was more important to the U.S. to resist communism than to promote their freedom. Unquestionably, it was right for those responsible for our foreign relations to appreciate the dangers which could threaten the Western World if the Soviet Union were to become the dominating force in Africa. But to begin to react against this possibility during the early 1950's, when most of Africa had yet to achieve its freedom, was to view the communist threat completely out of proportion and to misread the nationalistic feelings of the Africans themselves. They did not want to exchange one colonial master for another. In 1953, when Mr. Dulles first spoke out on his policy toward Africa and colonialism, Africa was an ideological desert for routine communist agitation.

There were important reasons for this. In the first place, the communist movement normally needed an industrial background against which to promote class warfare between the workers and the bourgeoisie. But, at the time, Africa was generally devoid of industry and was largely classless. Secondly, Russian communism, based on an international working-class movement, was totally incompatible with the African nationalist movements. In Black Africa, nationalism and independence were all one and the same thing. The Africans needed to promote nationalism and independence in order to win racial dignity, whereas the Soviets needed to destroy nationalism and independence in order to win international workers' dignity.

Finally, and perhaps the most critical factor keeping Africa out of reach of Soviet Russia, was the question of colonialism. Africa, in the wake of Asian independence, was in the process of escaping from European colonialism. At the same time, the Russians were endeavoring to maintain their own brand of colonialism. To accomplish this, the Russians needed a captive society, while the

Africans required a free society.

As a strategy, Stalin considered that he could circumvent these difficulties in Africa by injecting violence into the anti-colonial struggle. As noted before, the communists hoped to succeed in precipitating, in the colonies, a premature and disorderly independence which would leave the new nations so economically and politically weak that they could be speedily deprived of their new freedom and forcibly absorbed into the Soviet Union.

As it turned out, Stalin's strategy was not at all successful, but the thinking behind it revealed that the growing power of African nationalism, reinforced by the race issue, was being seriously underrated by the Russian leader as well as by the U.S. and some of its NATO allies. In his C.I.O. speech, Mr. Dulles had declared his concern that "Communists disguised as local patriots could take over the new governments." The fallacy, of course, was that this reasoning applied more properly to Russian take-overs in white, East European countries such as Poland, Czechoslovakia and Hungary. It was a pattern which simply could not be applied to nationalist progress in Africa. African nationalism was essentially a drive to get rid of white supremacy and colonial rule and no African leader in his right mind would have thought of transferring his people from the hands of one European master into the hands of another.

With the Asian examples already firmly in view, it was obvious that the success of African anti-colonialism was bound to follow. The only question was how soon. Conservative thinkers, such as the leaders of the Tory party in Great Britain and the corresponding leadership in both France and Belgium, believed in and wanted to retain the trappings, prestige and profits of empire.

They were unwilling to accept the long-range implications of the events of the day, such as the ferment in North Africa, the Mau Mau uprising in Kenya, and even the war in Indo-China. These thinkers and decision-makers tended to underrate the capabilities of the African leaders and to resist their demands for political progress. On the other side, those who were progressively inclined, like the British Labor Party, were anxious to avoid the violent situation which could arise if the momentum of

African nationalism was misjudged and resisted until it exploded. Considering American history and the past declarations of its political leaders, the U.S. should have been prepared to give its public sympathy and understanding cooperation to the Africans, who were determined to run their own affairs.

This might well have happened if the State Department and the Pentagon had made realistic appraisals of the strength and prospects of the world-wide campaign to end colonialism. An accurate assessment of whether European-directed communism could successfully penetrate and subvert the nationalist movement as it was developing throughout Africa was also lacking. Had such a long-range study been conducted, it could have been of enormous import. But, unfortunately, the State Department was European-oriented and not yet organized to pay the same degree of attention to Africa as it was to the other continents.

There was also another major weakness in U.S. policy toward colonialism. This was our failure to use political approach in favor of the Africans and the free world. The fact that we did not promote freedom as much as so many thought we should have was because we were overly fearful of communist methods and intentions. I believed that there are two principal ways to compete against aggressive communism. One is by military preparation and the other is by political maneuver. Obviously, both must be used, although in the end the latter can usually be the more effective.

But, however unintentionally, the U.S. downplayed the political weapon, both in Africa and at the U.N. By failing to use this important weapon, we gave the Soviet Union a free hand to press its attacks against colonialism without fear of response by the U.S. As a result, they were able to brand us a full-fledged member of that nefarious group. Even Stalin, in the planning of his African strategy, could not have hoped for such assistance, for it permitted the Russians to run political circles around the U.S.

This was particularly true at the U.N. where, time after time, the Russians enjoyed speaking and voting against colonialism, while we felt obliged to stand unenthusiastically with a tiny minority on the side of the colonial powers. Had we overcome our hesitation to irritate our NATO allies, we could have taken a pro-African position which would have been in keeping with our own traditions and would have put us in the unusual position of being in effect, a useful spokesman for both sides.

Our intervention on behalf of the Africans could have had many positive results. It could have helped to calm suspicion among them that independence might be indefinitely postponed. It could have injected a feeling of confidence into the nationalist movements. This, in turn, would have allowed them to concentrate more effectively on preparing for the responsibilities of independence rather than having to spend so much of their time organizing anti-colonial protest movements. It is not impossible that it might have quieted some of the discontent which had already brought on the terrible Mau Mau uprising, or that it might have induced the Belgians to help the Congo make better and more timely preparations for self-government and thus avoid the kind of political disintegration which followed its ultimate independence. Most of all, it would have unquestionably put a roadblock in the way of the strategic plans of the communists. All of these potential influences would have benefited both sides of the colonial issue. Many of them could have been brought about if we had given the Africans at least some support at the U.N.

By its very nature the U.N. is a political body and during this period would have provided an ideal forum in which the U.S. could play a more political role. As it was, the participation of the United States in the U.N. was handled by Ambassador Lodge, the former Senator from Massachusetts, with the greatest skill and foresight—except with regard for colonial matters. Through no fault of his, the U.S. Mission to the U.N. was under orders from Washington to stay on the side of the colonial powers. Admittedly, it would not have been easy for the U.S. to differ on colonial matters, but to do so would have been an act of statesmanship. In the long run it would have been a benefit to all the countries involved. In fact, a much better foundation for the international future of the U.S. might well have been laid had our foreign policy administrators in the State Department been responsive to the thinking of some of our most distinguished leaders.

At the time, Walter Lippmann made a very clear analysis of our realistic commitments under the NATO alliance. Referring to the strength and limitations of the alliance, he observed that:

> where the issue is national survival, the alliance is certain; where the issues are concerned only with national interests, there is not necessarily a common policy . . . [and] the allies could differ up to the point where the survival of any of them was threatened [in which case] the Atlantic community is bound together for the common defense by ties that are stronger than the terms of a treaty or the formula of a policy . . . [Short of that] the members have important interests which in varying degrees they regard as vital, that extend beyond the Atlantic community into the Pacific, into Asia and into Africa. Here there are differences as to what is vital, as to what should be done. . . . The unending task of diplomacy on both sides of the Atlantic is to see that when the allies diverge, they do not separate. . . . In the long run the cardinal task of the Atlantic Alliance is to work out a new relationship between the Atlantic community and the nations which are emerging from colonial status. . . . It is our interest, it is our duty . . . it is our mission to be at once ally of the West and its principal mediator, seeking the accommodations by which the liberation of the subject peoples can be accomplished without precipitating a world war.

It is also pertinent and revealing that General Eisenhower in his memoirs some years later, observed that:

> our deep conviction about colonialism has often brought us embarrassment in dealing with our friends in Western Europe, whose history as colonialists was largely alien to

our history. But the standing of the U.S. as the most powerful of the anti-colonial powers is an asset of incalculable value to the free world.

Another policy failure was the self-defeating efforts of the State Department to try to reconcile the official pro-colonial position of the U.S. with its anti-colonial past by devising a formula which could satisfactorily bridge the gap. This was advanced by Mr. Dulles in his C.I.O. speech of 1953 when he asserted that there would be "no slightest wavering in our [U.S.] conviction that the *orderly* transition from colonial to self-governing status would be carried *resolutely* to a completion."

This statement, which emphasized "orderly" and "resolutely," sounded good but meant nothing to the Africans, because we did nothing to back it up, preferring to leave the questions of decolonization entirely in the hands of the colonial powers. But it was a formula which was repeated almost word for word, again and again, through most of the decolonizing period.

It was used first by Assistant Secretary of State Byroade on October 31, 1953, in a speech which was very perceptive in its understanding and analysis of the feelings of the colonial peoples and their problems. However, it was so circumscribed with admonitions against the perils of communism and premature independence that it became a sort of general defense for almost any policy that any colonial power might pursue, either then or in the future. Mr. Byroade paraphrased Mr. Dulles' formula by stating that "much blood and treasure might be saved if the Western World determines firmly to hasten [meaning to press resolutely forward] rather than hamper the process of orderly evolution towards self-determination."

By way of explanation he warned that, in the name of independence [Soviet colonialism] persuades people to surrender all hope of independence, and that the U.S. does "not want the vast labor and pain in the struggle for freedom to be wasted by the premature creation of a state that will collapse like a stack of cards at the first hint of difficulty." He therefore suggested that, "if a few additional years of evolution can make the difference between a self-determination that endures and a reversion to dependency [this time under the Russians] . . . the years will not be wasted."

In short, although the speech pleaded to the contrary, it was open to the interpretation of being an excuse for delaying self-determination and as such was bound to cause disappointment among all the influential leaders of Africa. It provided the basic arguments which could support the colonial side of almost any debate which might arise in the U.N. and reaffirmed the Dulles formula which, in spite of its fulsome praise of self-determination and independence, placed the U.S. squarely in line to act as public advocate for the colonial powers. It certainly tied our hands in advance and made any subsequent change of policy more difficult.

Another speech of the same nature was delivered two years later by Under Secretary of State Robert Murphy, a senior member of the Foreign Service, who had served with such distinction in World War II and later as Ambassador to Belgium and Japan. Mr. Murphy gave a brilliant analysis of the technical problems involved in self-determination and the structure of a new nation.

Here again the theme of the speech concentrated on the Dulles formula of pressing resolutely for orderly progress toward self-government. Mr. Murphy's manner of expression was even more cautious than that found in the Byroade speech. He expressed the belief that the application of the principle of self-determination would doubtless continue to demand the attention of statesmen far into the future. He curiously considered that independence, particularly in Africa south of the Sahara, would be a very long time in coming. He spoke of the perplexing problems of how to determine "what is a 'people'? How large a group is it and how is it tied together?"

He spoke of the difficulty of "how we are to define a nation?" and of the problem of determining when it would be practical to apply the principle of self-determination. His tendency was to apply more restrictions to the development of nationhood in Africa than had been previously applied to the Asian nations—and indeed to the European ones—which had recently won independence. As an answer to the problems raised, he declared that the U.S. was prepared to bring before the General Assembly of the U.N., a proposal that the whole question of self-determination should be made the subject of a much more profound study to see if a substantial measure of agreement on the meaning and essential elements of the [independence] problem can be reached before adopting various other concrete proposals which have been presented to the Assembly.

After bringing out a number of further difficulties in the way of independence, Mr. Murphy concluded by affirming the Dulles formula that, in the interest of world peace and stability, we should recognize the necessity of proceeding in an *orderly* and *resolute* fashion in applying the principle of self-determination throughout the world.

The key words in this statement were identified by Mr. Murphy as "orderly" and "resolutely". The word "orderly," he said, implied that "a well-defined people or nation should have the opportunity to emerge into a status of self-government . . ., but that this status should not be undertaken prematurely, but at the same time [it should] be early enough so that violence is avoided." The word "resolutely" was used to explain that "the status should not be made subject to any undue delay."

By implication, this speech, along with most of the others which were delivered during this period, seemed to infer that if the U.S. became convinced that a given colonial power was not pressing resolutely toward the goal of self-government for its colonies, we would be ready to suggest to that power that it get on with the job. But there is no instance where such advice was publicly delivered. Except in the case of the International Trust Territories, the U.S. had no access whatever to knowledge of the internal workings of the colonial administrations. It was neither possible for our government to know what the colonial offices were planning in their inner councils, nor was it likely that our government would have criticized them publicly if it did.

Insofar as the Afro-Asian world was concerned, the

U.S. was tied to the coattails of our colonial allies and our efforts to preach in favor of political freedom were meaningless. To make matters worse, the U.S. was tied, not merely to the coattails of each ally, but to its most imperial faction, since each of these new governments was faced at home with strong anti-colonial opposition. In Great Britain, the colonial policy of the Tory government was constantly under attack by the Labor Party, especially in connection with colonies such as Kenya and Southern Rhodesia, which had important white-settler interests.

This division over colonial policy was equally true in France and ultimately in Belgium. In France, there was very heated disagreement between the conservative and liberal parties over their policies toward North Africa. The same heated arguments over colonial policy took place later in Belgium during the disorderly events which accompanied the granting of independence to the Congo.

In a sense, the same division between liberal and conservative thinking existed in the United States, except that the great bulk of American public opinion had traditionally been most liberal on the question of colonialism, whereas the policy of Mr. Dulles was extremely conservative, due principally to his overrating of communist possibilities in Africa. The result was that under his leadership the political position of the U.S. government toward Africa was, in effect, made for it by the most conservative political leaders in the colonial offices of Europe.

Another aspect of the U.S. alignment with the colonial powers was the damage it did to the good will that our country had previously enjoyed in the Afro-Asian world. Heretofore, these people had placed great faith in the meaning of the American Revolution and the Bill of Rights and the great declarations concerning liberty which were made by Thomas Jefferson and Abraham Lincoln.

Many years later, when President Wilson called for the "self-determination of all peoples," his declaration set men's minds on fire all over the world. During World War II, the Atlantic Charter, which was stimulated by the U.S., proclaimed that "the right of all peoples to choose a government under which they will live," is undeniable.

This concept was strongly championed by President Franklin D. Roosevelt, whose anti-colonial views once caused him to remark that, "when we win this war, I will work with all my might and main to see to it that the U.S. is not wheedled into the position of accepting any plan that will further France's imperialistic ambitions, or that will aid or abet the British Empire in its imperial ambitions."

It was no wonder that there was concern and disillusionment among the Afro-Asian leaders everywhere when the traditional anti-colonialism of the U.S. was so unexpectedly reversed. It was not as if the Afro-Asian people were merely an unimportant and underdeveloped corner of the world for, compared to the relatively small number of white people, the Afro-Asian world of color comprises the vast majority of mankind and faces a destiny that will one day give its people a decisive position in international affairs. This means that, in the long run, the white minority population of the Western World cannot continue to advance peacefully and materially unless it succeeds in winning the confidence and the cooperation of the Afro-Asian world.

This was put very clearly by James Reston of the *New York Times* during the early days of the Nixon administration when he observed that:

> In the [present] world almost all the rich nations are predominantly white and all the poorest nations are colored, and the rich white nations are a small minority of the human family, and the income gap between the rich nations and the poor nations is getting wider with every passing year. The danger of these facts is obvious.
>
> Moreover . . . the colored peoples are beginning to understand that poverty is not inevitable but intolerable, and that the real danger of the [future] may very well be that the conflicts of . . . international politics may not be ideological but racial.

Although it was not recognized at the time, perhaps

the greatest damage caused by our about-face on colonial issues was the loss of the idealism that had characterized so much of U.S. policy throughout its history. Even if such slogans as "the war to end all wars" or "to make the world safe for democracy" were failures in the end, the idealism which they suggested has almost always been an essential ingredient of American political aims. President Nixon was to say:

> Sceptics do not build societies. The idealists are the builders, and only societies that believe in themselves can rise to their challenges . . . When a nation believes in itself that nation can perform miracles. Only when a nation means something to itself can it mean something to others. That is why I believe in a resurgence of American idealism.

Without this idealism, especially in the eyes of the Afro-Asians, the American people were out of character and the task of representing our government in the Trusteeship Council became difficult and frustrating.

If our standing in the Afro-Asian world was damaged by our policy of unquestioning cooperation with our Colonial allies, this policy ironically did nothing to win us friends among these same allies. The deeply-rooted, well-established, anti-colonial bias of public opinion in the U.S. continued to arouse fierce resentment, especially among the Imperial-minded factions which were in office in all the members of NATO.

It caused some of their spokesmen to claim that the U.S. itself was a nation with colonial responsibilities abroad and racial injustices at home. It is true that we have had colonies but, except in the case of Alaska, the Hawaiian Islands, Puerto Rico and the Philippines, our dependencies have consisted mostly of some tiny islands in the Pacific which were seized from Japan in World War II and most of which contained less people than would be found in a small American village. Alaska and Hawaii were seeking to become American states in the early 1950's, and were in the final stages of being accepted into the Union. The Philippines had become independent in 1946. And in 1953 Puerto Rico, on its own initiative, was declared by the U.N. to be a self-governing Commonwealth associated with the U.S. President Eisenhower even promised it full support should it ever request independence. Without such assurance concerning independence, which was strongly recommended to the President by Ambassador Lodge and urgently favored by myself, the self-governing motion would have been voted down by the U.N. This would have had the effect of branding that country internationally as a colony of the U.S., embroiling us further with the unliberated Colonial world.

The example of the Philippines was another case of particular significance because it assumed independence according to a promise given to it by the U.S. Congress in 1936. The success of this procedure, under which the Philippine people knew ten years in advance when they would become independent, provided a tested base from which the U.S. could have projected a policy toward nationalist Africa which would have been consistent with its record in favor of self-determination. In other words, if the U.S. had adopted a policy tied to the use of timetables and target dates for self-government, the good will which had existed for the U.S. over so many years through much of the world, might have been preserved— at least until the war in Indo-China. And if, contrary to all likelihood, the idea of target dates could have been sold to the colonial powers, it might have eased some of the tension within the nationalist movements and provided more time for the African leaders to prepare for the inevitable problems of self-government.

The idea of promoting a central proposal to fix a time limit within which to complete the decolonization of Africa could well have been applied to almost all the trust territories, colonies and protectorates.

The French position in North Africa, however, would have raised certain problems which might have led the French to resist the idea of a target date for independence. Although the inevitability of early post-war independence for the Protectorates of Morocco and Tunisia was foreseen by most nations in the U.N., the situation in Algeria was much more complicated. Algeria was originally put together by France and was theoretically governed, not as a colony, but as an integral part of the French Republic. From both an economic standpoint and the needs of NATO, the continuance of French Algeria was widely considered by France as vital to its very existence. There was also the contention that Algeria came under the proviso of Article 2(7) of the U.N. Charter, which forbade the U.N. to intervene, or to consider any matters falling within the domestic jurisdiction of any member of the U.N. Accordingly, it did not appear illogical at first for the U.S. to argue in the U.N. that Algeria was to France as Texas was to the U.S. The flaw in this analogy was ultimately exposed when it became obvious that Algeria could no longer be divested of its geographical and political association with all overseas colonies in Africa; and, more particularly, of its position between the borders of Morocco and Tunisia. It was, in fact, a colony pure and simple, with all the unhappy accompaniments of "white supremacy" and the other inequalities of position and opportunity which separated the Europeans from the Algerians.

One of the first to put Algeria into proper perspective with all the other nationalist movements in Africa was Senator John F. Kennedy. As chairman of the Senate's Foreign Relations subcommittee on U.N. Affairs, Senator Kennedy delivered a remarkable speech which was highly critical of France in Algeria and of U.S.-African policy in general. Although it was not made until 1957, it revealed most effectively the inadequacies which bedeviled U.S. policy throughout the decolonization years.

In this address, Senator Kennedy contended that:

> The most powerful single force in the world today is neither communism nor capitalism, neither the H-bomb nor the guided missile . . . it is man's eternal desire to be free and independent. The great enemy of that

tremendous force of freedom is called, for want of a more precise term, imperialism . . . Thus the single most important test of American policy today is how we meet the challenge of imperialism, what we do to further man's desire to be free. On this test more than any other, this nation shall be critically judged by the uncommitted millions in Asia and Africa . . . If we fail to meet the challenge of . . . imperialism, then no amount of foreign aid, no aggrandizement of armaments, no new pacts or doctrines or high-level conferences can prevent further setbacks to our course and our security . . . I am concerned . . . that we are failing to meet the challenge of imperialism . . . and thus failing in our responsibilities to the free world.

With regard to Algeria and the war which was then being waged against France, the Senator observed that:

American and French diplomats have joined in saying for several years that Algeria is not even a proper subject for American foreign policy debates or world consideration . . . that it is wholly a matter of internal French concern, a provincial uprising . . . But, whatever the original truth of these cliches may have been, the blunt facts of the matter today are that the changing face of African nationalism, and the ever-widening by-products of the growing crisis, have made Algeria a matter of international concern, and consequently American concern.

The war in Algeria, engaging more than 400,000 French soldiers, has stripped the continental forces of NATO to the bone . . . It has repeatedly been appealed for discussion to the U.N., where our opposition to its consideration . . . [has] affected our standing in the fight to keep that world free, our prestige and our security. It has furnished powerful ammunition to anti-western propagandists throughout Asia and the Middle East.

In further comment he went on to say that there was not:

> . . . any value in the kind of discussion which has characterized . . . U.S. consideration of [colonial] problems . . . tepid encouragement and moralizations to both sides, cautious neutrality on all real issues, and a restatement of our obvious dependence upon European friends, our obvious dedication nevertheless to the principles of self-determination, and our obvious desire *not* to become involved. We have deceived ourselves into believing that we have thus pleased both sides and displeased no one with this head-in-the-sands policy . . . when, in truth we have earned the suspicion of all.
>
> This is not a record to view with pride . . . No matter how complex the problems posed . . . may be, the record of the U.S. [is] a retreat from the principles of independence and anti-colonialism, regardless of what diplomatic niceties, legal technicalities or even strategic considerations are offered in its defense . . .
>
> Instead of abandoning African nationalism to the anti-Western agitators and Soviet agents who hope to capture its leadership, the U.S., a product of political revolution, must redouble its efforts to earn the respect and friendship of nationalist leaders.
>
> If we are to secure the friendship of the Arab, the African and the Asian . . . and we must, despite what Mr. Dulles says about our not being in a popularity contest . . . strength[en] our appeal to these key populations . . . and it is rightfully our appeal, and not that of the Communists . . . [it] lies in our traditional and deeply felt philosophy of freedom and independence for all peoples everywhere.

I should point out in conclusion of this topic that this was a very difficult period for me and I was frustrated at having to constantly subordinate my own views to those of the State

Department, particularly as I considered those of Secretary of State Dulles to be incorrect and ultimately detrimental to the best interests of the United States.

At the same time, I would like to express my appreciation to Ben Gerig, my very able deputy on the Trusteeship Council, for he had to deal with my frustration on a regular basis, particularly as it related to my speeches before the Council. My statements had to be approved by the various divisions of State in Washington, especially the elite European division. This meant that, by the time everyone had had a chance to eliminate anything controversial or in opposition to their position, the speech itself often became dull and meaningless. It also made it very difficult for me to deliver them when everybody had reduced them to banal generalities and totally innocuous prose.

Dr. Nnamdi Azikiwe, Premier of Eastern Nigeria, greeting Mr. Mason Sears, U.S. Representative to the Trusteeship Council, at a reception at the Waldorf-Astoria, New York, arranged by the Nigeria Liaison Office.

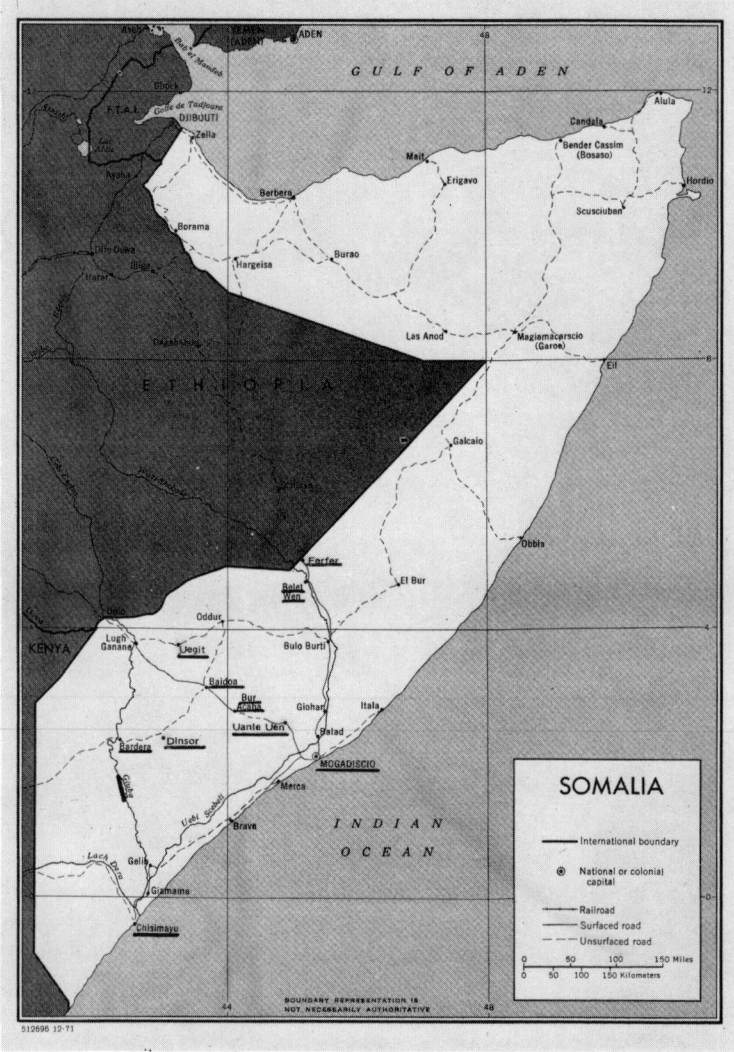

1954 Visiting Mission to Somalia.
Itinerary underlined.

Chapter VI

The Surge of Events

$\mathbf{D}$uring the three years following the 1954 Mission's visit to East Africa, the surge of events all across the continent demonstrated a continuous nationalist progress throughout Africa. During this period I was President of the Trusteeship Council for one year. On the occasion of my assumption of the Presidency, I made a short speech introducing certain views which I believed to be of importance because of their bearing on nationalist progress in Africa and other Trust Territories. I declared:

> It looks as if the Trusteeship Council faces a year of high purpose and great interest.
> For the first time we will be concerned with the mechanics of territorial self-determination.
> There are also other developments of an extremely important nature to be considered.
> This will involve two missions to West Africa in the autumn.
> A special mission will go to British Togoland to find out how Togolanders can best express their wishes about uniting with the Gold Coast upon its independence, which may come next year.
> This will probably lead to the first popular

referendum under the international trusteeship system.

Another mission will go to the British Cameroons, where there may be a second referendum in the near future in connection with prospective Nigerian independence.

These missions will be most important because West African developments are going to be followed with the closest attention throughout Africa.

At all events, the Council, operating as the eyes and ears of the United Nations, may be expected to play an increasingly useful role in the progress of trust territories towards self-government.

In the Pacific we operate at the center of the adjustment of formerly isolated peoples to a rapidly contracting world.

Some people, like those in New Guinea, are just emerging from isolation and from a condition of almost perpetual tribal warfare.

Others, like those in Western Samoa, are considering the form of self-government most suitable to their society.

This speech attracted considerable attention in Africa and numerous favorable comments. A few days later, I was particularly gratified to receive the following letter from Prime Minister Nkrumah:

21 June, 1955

Dear Mr. Sears:

The news of your election as President of the United Nations Trusteeship Council has just reached me, and I hasten to send you my heartiest congratulations on your election to this high office. As you have said yourself, the Trusteeship Council faces a year of high purpose and great interest; we in the Gold Coast are looking forward to the forthcoming Visiting Mission to Togoland under British and French Trusteeship.

> I should like you to accept the sincerest
> good wishes in your task not only from myself but from
> my Government and people of the Gold Coast and
> Togoland under United Kingdom Trusteeship.
>
> Yours very sincerely,
> (signed) Kwame Nkrumah
> Prime Minister

Unfortunately, because the U.S. was backed so firmly into the corner of the conservative elements of its European allies, it lost many important opportunities to exert both a stabilizing and friendly influence upon so many nationalist situations. Yet, paradoxically, it was President Eisenhower who threw aside a policy of treating our NATO allies with kid gloves. Especially in 1956, he took measures to bring to an abrupt halt the attempt of Britain, France and Israel to invade Egypt in order to repossess the Suez Canal.

Morocco, Tunisia and the Sudan had all won their independence and the fighting in Algeria continued its seemingly intractable course with no end in sight. Partly as a result of these events in the countries south of the Sahara, the demands of the nationalist leaders had become so insistent that, for the sake of law and order, the colonial administrators were forced to grant political concessions much more rapidly than had been intended. In fact, many of the French territorial administrators granted great freedom of action to their respective territories, perhaps with the anticipation that the Africans would be incapable of completing their tasks and would thus be forced to fall back on their French administrators, locking them into overseas France and preserving the French empire.

At this time, my wife and I journeyed through some of the affected areas all the way from Capetown to Timbuktu. It was our first trip to South Africa and we found it a beautiful but tortured land. We found white people's hatred of Africans, Afrikaner hatred of English-speaking people, and African fear and hatred of whites. The hatred which existed between the races was so great that one wondered how it was possible for such a cruel and divided society to exist in the 20th century.

At the bottom of the social, political and economic order came the black Africans, who were not allowed to unionize or to earn enough to escape from a subsistence livelihood. Next in line came the colored people, people of mixed racial background who, because they had some white blood in them, were permitted to earn more income for the same work that was done by the Africans.

Yet, ironically, the status of being colored was dubious and cruel in that family after family was split up as some members were classified white, some African, and some colored.

In addition to the Africans and the colored, there were Indians, who were segregated in the various towns in which they lived, but had none of the white man's privileges. On the top was the white minority, divided between the Dutch Boer farmers and the successful British businessmen.

One of the harshest features of the South African society was the requirement that all Africans carry a number of special permits, called passes, permitting them to do business either as domestics in the city or as farm laborers in the country. Day after day, thousands upon thousands of Africans who failed to be able to produce a pass card would be imprisoned. I shall never forget what I saw one day while traveling on a railroad from Mozambique to Johannesburg. When the train stopped at some unknown station, a long line of Africans, roped one to another presumably for minor pass infringements, was being led by the police onto the train. The most pathetic part of it were the poor wives who insisted on accompanying their men with whatever small possessions they owned until they had to leave their men with the authorities. These Africans were permitted to leave prison if they were willing to work for the pathetically low pay on the farms of the whites.

In short, South Africa was a land of racial hatreds, and the dislike of the Dutch farmer for the British businessman was so acute that I felt compelled to ask a distinguished British scholar whether the real danger was that racial conflict would break out between the white minorities rather than between the whites and the coloreds or Indians.

My friend, however, was quick to disagree with this view. He felt that the real threat came, not between the white people, but from the preponderance of blacks over whites should any violence break out. Yet, historically, the British settlers and the Afrikaners had fought for possession of South Africa and the long and bloody Anglo-Boer war left many scars on the white community.

In Johannesburg, the gold-mining center of Africa, we found teams of white recruiters traveling from country to country enlisting Africans for work within the mines. Africans so recruited were not permitted to bring their families and were consigned to compounds until their contracts expired.

One of the few outlets for relaxation in the mining compounds came on Sunday, when a series of tribal dances were held which were nothing short of fascinating to observe. Europeans and Africans alike, never failed to be on hand to watch these affairs. Most of them reflected the music and dancing of various tribes throughout Southern Africa.

There was one final aspect of conditions in South Africa which disturbed me very much. This was the failure of our Embassy in Pretoria to invite South African Blacks to its 4th of July celebrations. I reported this unsatisfactory situation to Ambassador Lodge because I felt that the barring of Blacks from these celebrations could have serious implications for the U.S. As public knowledge of this situation could be politically embarrassing at home, Ambassador Lodge dispatched the following letter to Secretary of State Dulles:

February 15, 1956

Dear Foster:

Herewith is the report which Mason Sears, the United States Representative on the Trusteeship Council, has made as a result of his recent trip to Africa.

I hope you will put it with those things which you plan to read when you get a chance because I believe it is well worth reading.

In particular, I invite your attention to what he says about the fact that American Embassies and Consulates in the Union of South Africa do not invite any colored persons to the Fourth of July celebration, and only invite a few in Kenya. The Soviets apparently do invite colored people and, according to him, it is by no means certain—even in the Union of South Africa—that all whites would refuse to come if we did the same.

I am worried about this thing from the standpoint of home politics. Recent events in Alabama create an exceedingly embarrassing issue for the Democrats. They would certainly jump on the Fourth of July business if they knew about it. *Per contra*, we could get some credit at home if we ended this practice. I can't help wondering whether our people are pushing the issue as hard as the traffic will bear, or merely following the line of least resistance.

****

Mason Sears may have irritated a few of the hard-shelled colonialists (although he is on very good terms with the actual administrators), but he certainly has made a lot of friends for us with the [Africans], who have the future in front of them and where it means something to the United States for the long pull.

Professor Edwin S. Munger, the American professor at Stellenbosch University in the Union of South Africa, in a letter written December 29, 1955, says: "Over the past ten months I've seen, I suppose, twenty more or less distinguished visiting firemen come to Stellenbosch for a day . . . May I say that no one has (1) gotten down to brass tacks better and really learned more and (2) left, as a liberal, a better impression behind him."

I think Sears' recommendations are well worth careful Department study.

Faithfully yours,

Henry Cabot Lodge, Jr.

The Honorable
  John Foster Dulles,
    Secretary of State.

When he did not receive a reply from Secretary Dulles, Ambassador Lodge dispatched a second letter on March 23:

Two Park Avenue,
New York 16, New York,
March 23, 1956.
PERSONAL
Dear Foster:
Herewith something from the "American Desk": In view of our election and the political situation, it is very important that our Ambassador and Consuls to the Union of South Africa should be told so to organize matters that it cannot be said that at our Fourth of July receptions in South Africa no colored people are invited.

I have written you already about this and had intended to speak to you at the Cabinet meeting, but did not get the chance.

I do not recommend that we advertise the fact that we are changing the policy. I simply recommend that we make the necessary changes so that we cannot be accused of excluding Africans from this celebration.

If we do not do so, I am afraid that we can get some extremely damaging publicity which will tend to rescue the Democrats from the terrible dilemma in which they find themselves, and which, if we make no mistakes, is bound to get worse.

It was a delight to see you looking so well after this trip.

With all good wishes,
Faithfully yours,

Henry Cabot Lodge, Jr.

The Honorable
John Foster Dulles,
Secretary of State.

A few weeks later, Ambassador Lodge received the following reply from Secretary Dulles:

April 3, 1956

Dear Cabot:

I read with interest your letter of March 23rd, as I had previously read your February 15th letter enclosing Mason Sears' report.

I entirely agree that invitations should not be issued on a basis of caste, color or creed at any of our public functions, either here or abroad. This is a good American principle that should guide all of us, all the times.

As regards the applicability of this principle to specific posts abroad, I believe our people should apply it to the extent the traffic will bear. The equally American characteristic of good common horse sense should also apply.

Thanks for bringing the matter to my attention.

Sincerely,
John Foster Dulles
The Honorable
  Henry Cabot Lodge, Jr.,
    The Representative of the United States,
      of America to the United Nations,
        Two Park Avenue,
          New York 16, New York.

This letter is of more than passing interest because it reveals Secretary Dulles' desire always to protect himself by being on both sides of an issue. But it seems inconceivable that Secretary Dulles would agree that invitations to the Embassy celebrations should not be based on caste, color, or creed, while at the same time intimating strongly that the application of such a principle could apply to current practice depending upon "what the traffic will bear". Obviously, it was utterly impossible for American policy to straddle both sides of this delicate issue. As a result, nothing was done to correct this situation until some years later, when our South African Embassy was finally required to invite Black Africans to participate in all celebrations held by American officials.

From South Africa, my wife and I traveled to Salisbury in Southern Rhodesia, where Mr. Garfield Todd was Prime Minister. Mr. Todd was a former missionary and was able to speak an African language. I had many talks with Mr. Todd, who clearly recognized that time was running out for the white man and that Southern Rhodesia would probably be unable to preserve its status as a semi-autonomous republic for more than a dozen years. Rhodesian society was strictly segregated and the city of Salisbury would not permit the only European-trained African doctor to live within the confines of Salisbury, the city in which he practiced. Instead, he was required to live within the African location some distance away. At this time in Salisbury, no Africans were allowed to enter the British-run shops. They could only stick their faces through a slot in the side of the wall and ask for what they wanted, but it was strictly forbidden for them to physically enter a shop.

At that time, Rhodesia consisted not only of Southern Rhodesia, which was a colony, but also the protectorates of Northern Rhodesia and Nyasaland. Under protectorate treaties they could not remain forever under British supervision and I made sure that this relationship was not forgotten in official circles.

It was the custom of the British government to keep the State Department informed of its policies for Rhodesia. I always sat and listened until the end of the discussion, then would make it a point to ask the British representative to reassure us that the British government had no intention of breaking its protectorate treaties with Northern Rhodesia and Nyasaland. As a result, Sir Andrew Cohen, who was the British representative on the Trusteeship Council, reaffirmed on at least half a dozen occasions that the British government had no intention of evading its protectorate responsibilities.

After visiting Salisbury, we traveled to both the protectorates of Northern Rhodesia and Nyasaland. In Nyasaland, disturbances had been the order of the day for some time. These disturbances centered around Dr. Kamuza Banda, who had practiced medicine for some years in California. The desire to get him to return to Nyasaland to take over the nationalist affairs of his people was so strong that he was elevated to the status of national hero. We were fortunate enough to arrive shortly after he had returned to support his people. When we called upon him, we found him living in very simple quarters, practicing medicine, assisted by a single nurse. But he was kind enough to give us several extended interviews.

This was a dangerous time for Europeans in Blantyre, the capital. However, we must have struck up more of a friendship than I realized at the time, for a few months later, after he was imprisoned by the British authorities, he sent word that he wished to have his regards conveyed to me. I was glad to receive a message like this as it indicated that he understood that I represented the true disposition of the American people. There was nothing I could do except to thank him for his message and to send some books and magazines to him in jail.

From Nyasaland we paid a short visit to Northern Rhodesia. It was very encouraging to find that the Governor of Nyasaland and the Governor of Northern Rhodesia were both liberal and forward-looking men who understood and sympathized with African nationalism. In fact, the Governor of Nyasaland and the Governor of Northern Rhodesia were cut from the same cloth as the brilliant Governor Sir Charles Arden-Clarke of the Gold Coast.

After a brief stop in the Congo, we flew from Leopoldville directly to Accra, where we had the opportunity to hire a car and travel deep into the interior of the Northern Gold Coast. There we stayed with and received the kindest hospitality from the Provincial Commissioner, Mr. MacDonald-Smith.

From the Gold Coast, we traveled to Bamako in Mali, where we boarded a large boat on the Niger River. The Niger becomes navigable only when it gets so wide in places as to remind one of the Mississippi River in the spring. The object of the voyage was to transport people and supplies to some of the most interesting cities of interior Africa.

The purpose of the trip for my wife and I was to observe life in this part of the African interior and especially to have a short visit to the famous city of Timbuktu. There were frequent stops made by the boat for the purpose of discharging passengers and supplies at the various river ports. These ports had the most colorful names—Koulikoro, Segou, Dia Farabe, Mopte, and Niafunke. The boat never stopped for more than a few hours at a time but during its stay it discharged and took on cargo and was the object of curiosity which attracted crowds of Africans to watch the vessel being loaded and unloaded. Most of the towns had huge mosques which gave one the feeling of being caught in a dream of the Arabian Nights. However, despite the dream-like atmosphere of these places, they were as busy as any good-sized American town.

On our trip along the river we saw many dugouts powered by American-made outboard motors, which had been redesigned to fit into the long, narrow dugouts that plied the river. At every stop we received the kindest of hospitality from the various French official residents. These officials were invariably army officers. Many of them seemed very homesick. Yet, on other occasions, we learned that for some reason the call of the desert was for these Frenchmen the same as the call of the open sea for the British.

Three or four miles inland by way of rough pathways and sand dunes, we came to the famous city of Timbuktu. The city was little more than a shell of its fabled past. The buildings were there, but the population had long since diminished. Just outside of the city limits was a huge French fort and in the marketplace the areas were full of camels resting after having deposited huge slabs of salt, which were piled up neatly at certain points of the marketplace. To many Frenchmen, living at Timbuktu, it must have seemed that they could not be living further away from any kind of life or home that they had known before.

Upon leaving Timbuktu, we traveled downstream, as far as the town of Gao. From there we took a plane which stopped at numerous places, permitting us to get out and talk with the people. In all these visits my wife's knowledge of French enabled me to communicate with the African officials. In almost every case, whether it was on the river banks or on the airplane journey to

French Guinea, we found that the framework of self-government had already been established.

It was around this time that the French Parliament had enacted the *Loi-Cadre*. This law gave most of French Equatorial and West Africa a further degree of self-government, but not pure independence. All the French territories voted to accept the privileges of the *Loi-Cadre*, with the exception of French Guinea, which, under the aggressive leadership of Sekou Toure, flatly refused to accept less than the total independence of his country. This refusal so enraged the French authorities that they immediately left the country *en masse*, stripping their offices of all furniture and equipment which could be used by the Africans to re-establish the governmental structure.

Our next visit was to Uganda, which was under the liberal leadership of Sir Andrew Cohen. The situation in Uganda was complicated by the fact that a majority of its people were Buganda and had little or no interest in the chiefs and members of the smaller tribal groups. Trouble had arisen in Uganda early in the 1950's, when the Kabaka demanded full independence for the Buganda. There followed a degree of unrest which was quite threatening. On one occasion, Sir Andrew's motorcar became a target of so many rocks and stones that he had to lie on the bottom of the car for protection as he traveled through the affected areas. In due course, the political situation became more relaxed and it became possible for the British government to maintain a less punitive attitude toward the Uganda protectorate. Eventually, the British decided that it would be wise to return the Kabaka from the exile they had imposed upon him when he pushed too strongly for independence for the Buganda.

As it happened, the day before his plane was to land in Uganda, my wife and I arrived at Entebbe, the port city for Kampala, where we were surprised but delighted to receive a message from Governor and Lady Cohen, inviting us to supper. There were no other guests, which made the occasion the more interesting in that Sir Andrew was able to candidly explain to us the political situation which then existed.

When our plane had arrived at Entebbe the day before,

we were impressed by the thousands of Africans who had come down to the airport to watch the arrival of plane after plane of British officials.

The following day, Sir Andrew invited my wife and I to accompany him to the Entebbe airport, where the Kabaka's plane was due to arrive. There, we were given seats next to the Kabaka's very pretty wife. When the plane finally arrived and the Kabaka had descended the steps to the runway, we were shocked to observe that he almost totally ignored his wife, from whom he had been separated during the period of his exile.

That night, we attended a large fair, where much celebrating was in progress, when suddenly a huge truck, driven by a man, obviously intoxicated, lurched through the crowd, narrowly missing many people. To my horror, the truck missed my wife by not more than a few feet before it bounced off into the darkness.

Sir Andrew was also kind enough to give us front row seats to ceremonies at the formal transfer of power back to the Kabaka. Prior to the Kabaka's arrival, Governor Cohen, who was attired in a full-dress diplomatic uniform covered with gold, continued to walk up and down, somewhat nervous as to what was to take place. His uniform was the last thing an already nervous man would want to wear in an already hot climate. The investiture, however, went off without incident, while outside huge Ugandan drums were beating in such a manner that it sounded like the rolling of thunder.

From Uganda, we traveled to Ethiopia, where the King of Kings, Haile Selassie, promised a new and more liberal constitution to the Ethiopian people. I was appointed by the Secretary of State as an official delegate to the celebrations. Haile Selassie's court was modeled after the high court of Sweden, which was the most formal court in Europe. The Ethiopian Court was conducted with the strictest formalities. This meant that when the members of the delegation and the Ambassador met with Haile Selassie to salute him on his silver jubilee, we were advised to wear tail coats.

The jubilee commemorating the new constitution

lasted for several days and involved visiting all kinds of farms and projects which the Emperor was carrying out in his country. One of the principal and most impressive events of the jubilee was the religious ceremony of the Coptic Church. It was higher than any church service of my experience and seemed to be a ceremony that had come down unchanged through the ages. In many instances, the participating clergy wore golden crowns and went through many forms of religious rites to the accompaniment of the usual beating of huge drums from outside the Cathedral.

There were many other occasions of great interest, including an exhibition by traditional dancers who, as they passed the grandstand, put on mock battles. Then came a large, modern, military parade in which the Emperor, dressed more like a British field marshal than an African Emperor, reviewed the various military units. The royal air force, consisting of a few dozen planes, passed overhead and the drumming, as usual, was superb.

The thing which interested me the most was the constant presence of the famous Galla horsemen. These cavalrymen were to be seen riding three abreast, all carrying guns or spears, and wearing lion headdresses. They made a very powerful impression on all who saw them. These men ride on saddles very similar to the American western saddle and are famous for their horsemanship.

Court life in Ethiopia was riddled with intrigue, so much so that I was shocked to learn a few years later that when the Emperor was absent from the country on a foreign visit, some of the dissident courtiers tried to dethrone him and install his son in his place. But the Emperor returned and restored order. The final event of the jubilee was the convocation of the Ethiopian parliament, at which the Emperor announced a new and more liberal Ethiopian constitution.

As we returned home, I felt that the surge of events, propelling African nationalism closer and closer to its goal of political independence, was gaining in strength and force and that its ubiquitous nature meant that the entire continent would soon feel its effects.

Chapter VII

The Birth of Ghana

1957 was a watershed year, one in which the pace of African independence quickened with the birth of the new nation of Ghana, the first black African state to attain independent status since World War II.

In December of 1957, Ghana celebrated its independence. President Eisenhower designated Vice President Nixon to head a delegation to attend the celebration ceremonies. The Vice President was kind enough to include me as one of the official members of his delegation. This journey turned out to be one of the most varied and interesting of my African experience.

During our flight across the Atlantic, I had the pleasure of enjoying cocktails and conversation with the Vice President and Mrs. Nixon, and the time passed quickly on the way to Morocco.

When our plane arrived, we were met by Crown Prince Hassan, who took the Vice President into a special reception room, where they had a formal drink of tea. After that, we were conducted to a long line of cars sufficient to accommodate all the members of Mr. Nixon's party. The Vice President and the Crown Prince were seated in their car and had just started on their way, when Mr. Nixon asked the chauffeur to stop, whereupon he got out of the car and shook hands with every member of the long line of Moroccan notables who had come to greet him. After this, the procession continued on its way.

As we travelled along, we noticed that at about one-mile intervals a Moroccan soldier was sitting on a camel. Each soldier would fire a rifle salute as we passed by. As we got into the city limits of Casablanca, the crowds became very thick. This was made to order for the Vice President who took frequent opportunities to stop the car, step out, and shake hands with the literally hundreds of Moroccans who swarmed around him to have a look and say hello. This happened time after time. From the reception we received it was quite clear that the United States stood high in the regard of the Moroccan people. It was an occasion which made us all proud.

The Vice President's visit to Africa could not have been more timely and the way he conducted himself made countless friends for the United States. His reception by hundreds of thousands of Moroccans was marked by extraordinary popular enthusiasm. I had the feeling that for once the United States had returned to its previous high standing which it had enjoyed before Secretary Dulles required us to become so strongly identified with European colonial powers. The Vice President was particularly effective in the way he mingled with the crowds in the streets and shook hands. It was said that he represented the first high-level official call which a non-African had made on the people of Morocco.

From Casablanca our plane flew to Accra, the capital of the new nation of Ghana. The Vice President's visit was very much appreciated by Prime Minister Nkrumah and the other leaders of the new government. One of the Cabinet Ministers told me that he was much impressed by the way Mr. Nixon shook hands with everyone who came to greet him on his arrival at the airport. He said it stood out in sharp contrast to the arrival of the Duchess of Kent who, on account of her royal position, was not permitted to shake hands indiscriminately.

From the airport we were taken to a new, modern hotel, where we stayed for the duration of our visit. The following day, the official delegation, headed by Mr. Nixon, made a formal visit to greet the new Premier, Kwame Nkrumah, and his right-hand man, Mr. Gbedemah. When it came my turn in line to shake hands, the Prime Minister was kind enough to thank me publicly for the stands I had taken in the Trusteeship Council when I supported the splitting of the Ewe tribe between the new state of Ghana and the small Trust Territory of Togoland. While this had caused considerable resentment among the Ewe's of Togoland, I could see no other rational solution of the so-called "Ewe problem".

I also had several conversations with Mr. Grunitzky, who was the African Prime Minister of the Trust Territory of French Togoland. On two occasions he gave me a very warm invitation to visit him in Lomé before I returned home but unfortunately I was unable to accept them.

While in Ghana I also talked with Mr. Sylvanus Olympio, who opposed the French-controlled government headed by Mr. Grunitzky. From sources which I believed reliable, I was told that Finance Minister Gbedemah had made available a sizable sum of money to Mr. Olympio for the purpose of assisting him in persuading the Ewe people of Southern Togoland to turn away from the French and join the new state of Ghana, which was to incorporate two-thirds of all the Ewe people. Mr. Olympio was reported to be undecided on how far he should pursue this matter.

The next day, when our delegation made a formal call upon the Prime Minister and his Cabinet, Mr. Casely-Hayford, Minister of Communications, who became the first Permanent Representative of Ghana to the United Nations, spoke to me of his liking for Americans. He was especially complimentary about the American GIs who were stationed in the Gold Coast during World War II. The sight of GIs digging ditches, carrying loads and doing other acts of manual labor impressed the Gold Coasters immensely. He said that the Americans, by their own example, had taught the average Ghanian the dignity of manual labor. He also said that the Africans enjoyed conversing with Americans because the Americans were willing to talk with them on any subject, whereas other people were inclined to be reserved.

Replying to a question concerning the conduct of the

independence celebrations, he felt that the British had somewhat overplayed the presence of the Duchess of Kent and that in preparing for the ceremonies, the Ghanian Cabinet had had to restrain the British from creating too much of a coronation atmosphere. I found the same reaction in many other Africans, who felt that it almost seemed as if Ghana was merely transferring from a Colonial status into some other form of subservience to the British Crown. In some ways this submerged the basic fact that the new nation had become as free and independent as Great Britain itself. At all events, Mr. Casely-Hayford was obviously very friendly towards Americans and was much pleased with the presence of the Vice President.

Several days of celebrations followed, featuring traditional dancing from the various tribes represented. Inevitably, there was a long list of receptions during which the Russian delegation was exerting every effort to win a place in the good will of the new state. They seemed to be meeting with mixed success.

When it came to the turn of the United States to hold its reception I was somewhat disturbed to find that no invitation had been extended to Julius Nyerere. This seemed but another instance of the lack of interest the State Department was displaying towards the rapidly developing nationalism of the African continent. I explained to Nyerere that this was an oversight and that he was expected. I asked him if he would accompany me in person to the festivities. This gave me the opportunity to introduce Nyerere to Vice President Nixon.

On March 6, the former Gold Coast and the Trust Territory of British Togoland united to become the first of the colonial peoples south of the Sahara to achieve their full freedom as an independent sovereign state. Although Prime Minister Nkrumah's life was to end in disappointment and exile, at the time of independence he made numerous statements of high purpose. Expressing the spirit and driving force of patriotism, for example, he declared:

In our daily lives we may lack those

material comforts regarded as essential by the standards of the modern world but we have the gifts of laughter and joy, a love of music, a lack of malice, an absence of the desire for vengeance for being wronged.

Another saying which has outlived him is "Seek ye first the political kingdom and all the rest shall be added unto you." And perhaps his most famous saying of all was: "We prefer self-government with danger to tranquility in servitude."

What impressed me most in speaking with Nkrumah and the other African nationalist leaders was the extent to which the issue of race so dominated their views. To me, it seemed particularly unfair that the British, who were doing such an excellent job of transferring power to their Colonial dependencies almost everywhere in the world, suffered from a lack of popularity.

This may have been due to an unconscious attitude of superiority which some of them possessed. On the other hand, I gained the feeling that Americans were accepted by Africans and Asians alike, as friends and equals, to whom they could freely speak without restraint. If this was an accurate reflection, and I believe it was, it was an American asset which we should have taken particular pains to preserve. This was especially true in Africa where, under the influence of the Algerian rebellion and the political situation in South Africa, the racial issue was coming more and more to the fore.

Before I departed Accra, I called on Governor General Sir Charles Arden-Clarke. He said that he was tired as an aftermath of the Celebrations and regretted that he was obliged to be so tied up during the period when the Duchess of Kent was in town. As I left, he made a remark which impressed me for its truth and simplicity and because it came from a man of such great experience who had just completed the safe, non-violent guidance of a new nation to independence. He remarked that in Africa "modern colonialism must be a partner of nationalism," although he did observe that this was easier in territories where there were no important communities of white people. Most certainly British colonial policy had achieved a first-rate partnership with nationalism in Ghana, Nigeria and the other parts of West Africa. However, the white minorities in East and Central Africa made this objective most difficult.

It appeared to me that the events accompanying the liquidation of European control in Africa would come with almost startling rapidity, even within four or five years. This being so, I believed that statements of United States policy concerning African affairs needed to be directed, more and more, along lines which would have indicated to the Africans that we had a deep interest in their future.

Obviously, this would not have been welcomed by the relatively small European minorities which had settled in Kenya, the Rhodesias and South Africa. However, there was very little middle ground in the racial issues of Africa. Thus, to risk offense to no more than 2½ million Europeans in Africa south of the Sahara, 80 percent of whom lived in the Union of South Africa, seemed a small price to pay in exchange for what might have been the last opportunity to win the confidence of 160 million Africans during the critical days in the evolution of their continent which was, and remains, so vitally important to the United States.

The chain reaction which followed the independence of Ghana spread throughout Africa. Time seemed speeded up by events. There were riots in Southern Rhodesia, Nyasaland, and in the Congo where 250 people were killed. The French decided to hold self-government plebiscites in all their Black African colonies. This was particularly interesting as the French elections were the first to be held under the terms of the Fifth French Republic as set up by DeGaulle. These plebiscites forecast an early independence for all of the French colonies in Black Africa.

The Algerian war was continuing in full force and some of the Algerian troops were infiltrating across the Tunisian border in order to enjoy temporary sanctuary. This brought on the tragic French bombing of independent Tunisia.

The most interesting event of 1958 was the All-African People's Conference, which was held in Accra with Nkrumah acting as the host. I was most anxious to observe first-hand the prevailing mood of nationalist Africa which was certain to be in evidence at this conference. With some difficulty I applied for an observer's seat from the credentials committee, none of whom I knew personally. Fortunately, Kodjo Botsio, Ghanian Minister of External Affairs, happened to put in an appearance in time to tell the Committee that "he is on our side." This produced a good seat enabling me to be present at and to hear all the conference speeches and events.

There were numerous communists from Egypt and even some from the Soviet Union. But most of them were not allowed by the Africans to take part in the proceedings. They were a noisy contingent on the floor, however, so that whenever a congratulatory message was read to the Conference from any of the communist countries, there was considerable clapping. To my chagrin, however, no message came from the United States and this omission was obviously used against the United States. How easy it would have been for our government to have sent a statement that we wished the Conference good luck in achieving those things which were needed for the success of Africa—a success which was richly deserved. But this omission again served merely to underscore the low priority which Africa was accorded by the State Department.

Both Tom Mboya of Kenya and Nkrumah reacted to the absence of official American greetings to the Conference. This hostile reaction to the American failure finally induced the American embassy in Accra to dispatch a message of congratulations. Unfortunately, the message from Vice President Nixon did not reach Prime Minister Nkrumah until the day the Conference closed. Although it helped to assuage some of the Africans' feelings, its lateness indicated a definite lack of interest by the American government. It also demonstrated a lack of sympathy with their aspirations for self-government. To me it was but another example of the need for greater acumen in the State Department in the area of African Affairs.

During the Conference I had many opportunities to talk with people who knew a great deal about Africa. A good many of them had reacted with favor to the stand I had taken in supporting the absorption of the Trust Territory of British Togoland into the new nation of Ghana. This was especially pleasing to me as my position on this matter followed along the lines of the U.S. policy of President Franklin Roosevelt and Secretary of State Cordell Hull when they insisted that there be special consideration of Trust Territories in the U.N. Charter itself. I followed this policy in the face of considerable criticism by some members of the State Department. Therefore, the positive reactions which I received from these Africans and other people knowledgeable of African affairs was most reassuring.

During the Conference I was asked to lunch by the American Ambassador, Mr. Flake. I found him to be inexplicably overcautious in his conversations with me. This did not disturb me at first but I was later somewhat taken aback when I learned that Andrew Lang, the Senior Foreign Service Officer attached to the Ambassador, had been chastised by him for showing me the confidential files of the Embassy. Previously, whenever I had visited an American Consulate or other diplomatic mission, I had always been shown all their files concerning the situation in Africa as they saw it. In the case of Ambassador Flake, however, poor Mr. Lang had received quite a lecture for having shown me any of the documents.

When I returned to New York, I suspected that there might be some criticism arising from my unauthorized presence at the All-African People's Conference. To my surprise and pleasure, Assistant Secretary of African Affairs Satterthwaite issued a statement in which he approved my attendance at the Conference.

As I indicated in previous chapters, it had become increasingly apparent that African nationalism was developing in the Belgian Congo. This forced a revolutionary reversal of Belgian policy which had always struggled hard to isolate the Congo from the nationalism that was sweeping across every other part of Africa. This flow of events finally forced the Belgian government to recognize that its policy of isolating the Congo from the rest of Africa was no longer viable. It finally became apparent to the Belgians that they were faced with the unpleasant alternatives of being forced to grant independence to their territories or to rule by force. Thus, both the

Belgian government and its Congolese opposition accepted the philosophy that only by being generous and forthright could Belgium possibly hope to maintain the good will of the Congolese people and thereby insure itself a special position in the independent Congo of the future.

In light of all these factors, the Belgian government finally agreed to grant independence to the Congo as of June 30, 1960. Some Belgians, including Governor-General Cornelis, thought for a while that the Congolese would be satisfied with only the word "independence" and would not insist on the real transfer of authority. But the Congolese representatives to the Brussels Conference made it clear that the Africans wanted full responsibility for governing themselves.

Since independence was scheduled to arrive only five months later, many Belgians felt that the political difficulties which were certain to arise would be enough to insure the postponement of independence for a substantial period. And, lacking any formal training or preparation for independence, the Congolese almost immediately broke into hostile internal factions. In the main, these were divided between the soon-to-be President, Kasavubu, whose fate later landed him in a Congo jail; the soon-to-be Prime Minister, Lumumba, the very powerful and influential nationalist; and Tshombe, who was determined to separate the copper-rich Katanga province from the rest of the Congo and make it independent on its own account. Ultimately, there was rioting in which hundreds of people were killed. These riots marked the end of a peaceful transition to independence almost as soon as it had begun. In fact, it was this absence of law and order which finally provided the U.N. with its impetus and reason for voting to send in a United Nations peace-keeping force. The collapse of Belgian policy over the years in the Congo was the classic example of misreading African nationalism.

Nationalism in Kenya was also becoming of greater and greater significance. During this period, the late 1950's to the early 1960's, Tom Mboya had become an inspiring and impressive nationalist leader and was making demands which the British government found it had to meet. The British government made an attempt to give more responsibility to Kenya and set aside a day on which Governor Baring was scheduled to make a progress statement to the Kenyan legislature. Because of its proximity and influence upon the Trust Territory of Tanganyika, I visited Nairobi for the purpose of being on hand when the Governor was to make his address. Due to the kindness which Mboya had shown me on a number of occasions, I was very pleased when he assigned me one of his seats in the gallery of the Legislature.

The entire event was a full-dress affair with the Governor appearing in full diplomatic uniform. It was expected that Governor Baring would announce new political advances for the Kenyan people. His speech proceeded as expected until he indicated a much slower pace of political advance. It was at this point that Tom Mboya, followed by most of the African members, arose from his seat and left the chamber.

From this experience, it was quite evident to me and to most of the members of the Trusteeship Council, that the unusual influence which the Kenya settlers had in London and which was responsible for many British policies in Kenya, might, in fact, act as a deterrent to peaceful political development and would always put the government at odds with the African majority. As a result I decided to make a speech in the Trusteeship Council which would express my fears as to the possible and probable results of this British policy.

In attempting to be as diplomatic as possible, I made the topic of my speech Tanganyika but I knew that those hearing the speech would be well aware of the implications for Kenya. Following long and patient tutoring by my friend and deputy, Ben Gerig, I was very careful to make an accurate statement but also one which would pull no punches and yet be acceptable to the State Department. Because of its sentiments and the objections to it which were raised by the British officials, I will take the liberty of quoting the speech in its entirety:

The Trusteeship Council in its

examination of conditions in Tanganyika cannot afford to overlook or to misunderstand the meaning of recent events in Africa or to underestimate the forces that underlie the primary African urge for freedom and equality. The Council, of course, has no responsibility for events outside the Trust Territory. But we know that a sympathetic understanding of the forces involved has now become more necessary than ever if the final phases of trusteeship in Tanganyika are to be successful. We also believe that the present administration in the Trust Territory is acutely aware of this.

Furthermore, if Tanganyika responds to the accelerating tempo of the times and achieves self-government smoothly and without delay, its example may have a constructive bearing on political stability and constitutional development in areas beyond its borders.

At all events almost overnight the affairs of Tanganyika and the role of the international Trusteeship System itself has taken on a new and unexpected significance for the future of Africa.

Like its neighbors, Tanganyika has a community of European settlers, who are very active in the political life of the Territory. Temporarily this community holds as many seats in the Legislative Council as the Africans, who outnumber them 2,000 to 1.

In such territories, two basic requirements must be met by the administration if effective and orderly progress toward independence is to be maintained.

The first is that there must be a clear understanding of the acceptance by the Africans of the political goals which they are headed for.

In Tanganyika one of the first acts of the new Governor Sir Richard Turnbull was to improve the political atmosphere by announcing that when self-government is attained both the legislative and executive sides of government are likely to be predominantly African.

This pronouncement, which is taken to mean that Tanganyika will be developed as a state primarily African in character and with a government mainly in African hands, had been urged for several years

115

by many voices in this Council including that of the United States.

We were glad to hear therefore that it was extremely well received in the Territory even though similar statements in less explicit language had been expressed on a number of occasions by the preceding administration. It should remove for all time the fear of those Africans who believed that their Territory was headed for a form of self-government which would allow Europeans to retain a disproportionate share of political control.

The second basic requirement is that Africans must have satisfactory evidence of the plans being made for their progress toward independence. In the often expressed opinion of the United States Delegation, this can best be accomplished by announcing from time to time the period within which the government hopes to accomplish the next step in its program leading toward self-government. We believe that such publicly planned, step-by-step progress gives to the people a sense of purpose and direction which will enable them to move more rapidly and more harmoniously ahead than might otherwise be possible.

In keeping with this philosophy the United States Delegation hopes that the government in the near future will consider the advisability of indicating an approximate date for the achievement of fully responsible ministerial government in the Territory.

The United States Delegation also hopes that the next territorial constitution will provide for universal suffrage. In our statement of last year we requested the Administering Authority to consider the advisability of such a step and we repeat the suggestion again this year.

The privilege of universal suffrage has been extended by the British Government to the people of its dependent territories in other parts of Africa. It was established by the French Government several years ago in all of the twelve territories in French West and Equatorial Africa. It will be established in limited form in the Congo this year and is already in operation in all African trust territories except Tanganyika.

If the establishment of universal suffrage

was advisable in all these places, ranging from territories in the remote interior to those on the coastline, it may also be helpful in Tanganyika. In any case, Tanganyika should not be held back because of official policy in adjoining territories.

This leads me to comment on the geographical fact that the Trust Territory lies between other territories in East and Central Africa where there are somewhat similar problems of adjustment between Africans and Europeans. The United States Delegation recognizes that there could be serious consequences for Africa if a possibly slower rate of political progress in these territories were somehow unintentionally permitted to slow down the faster rate of progress which could be expected under present circumstances in Tanganyika. However, there is no present indication that this will happen. The United States Delegation has confidence that the Administering Authority will encourage Tanganyika, as a Trust Territory, to advance on its own merits unimpeded by conditions in neighboring areas which are not under international supervision.

Mr. President, I shall not touch on the economic problems of the Territory except to say that our Delegation is glad to hear that the British Government has accepted the obligation to assist Tanganyika in meeting its budgetary deficit. Tanganyika will not be the first territory to start its independent life under financial difficulties. These can be overcome in time—especially if its eventual African government succeeds, as we think it will, in proving that it intends to do everything in its power to protect local enterprises and attract further investments from the outside world.

But aside from its economic handicaps, Tanganyika is fortunate in many ways.

Politically, for example, it is less divided between its nationalist and its traditional tribal leaders than most other territories. In this sense Tanganyika has a basic political unity which is as good or better than any other territory south of the Sahara.

In TANU—the Tanganyika African National Union—it also has one of the largest and most effective political organizations in Africa. TANU is already reported to have many hundreds of thousands of

Africans who have paid dues into its treasury.

I also believe that the Trusteeship Council will agree when I say that the leader of TANU, Julius Nyerere, is one of the ablest of the African spokesmen who have appeared before the United Nations. He, in turn, is assisted by many capable lieutenants, but could use many more.

In looking toward the future the United States Delegation hopes that this very influential organization will be encouraged to build up its internal strength and discipline. This is most important because much of Tanganyika's success or failure in the next few years will resolve around the activities of TANU.

Mr. President, before I close I would like to report that a visit to Dar es Salaam last November produced an impression that the new administration in Tanganyika had injected fresh life and a progressive atmosphere into the political affairs of the Territory.

The United States Delegation has high hopes that the final chapters in the dependent life of Tanganyika will be as successful as they have been in other territories which have been so successfully administered by the British government.

Despite taking great pains to insure that my statements were correct, my speech had a most unhappy effect on the British representative, Sir Andrew Cohen, whose seat was next to mine. He began to elbow my shoulder in annoyance with what I was saying until I had to stop and ask him to leave me alone so that I might complete my statement! At the end of my speech, Sir Andrew expressed his dissatisfaction with the points I had made, but said he would have to live with them. Strangely enough, it was the French and other delegations who informed my people that they thought it was time that the British should be talked to in that way.

In Tanganyika, there was also considerable irritation. I was informed that all the good will that I had struggled to develop in a previous visit had been destroyed. All of the facts in my speech had been carefully checked and were correct; it was therefore puzzling to try and explain why the speech met with such strong objections among the British people in Tanganyika. A copy of the statement was sent to the Governor of Tanganyika, Sir Richard Turnbull, a day prior to its release to local newspapers via the United States Information service.

This action was taken by Consul-General William (Red) Duggan, not only as a matter of courtesy, but also to make sure Sir Richard saw the full text. Immediately after the Governor saw the statement he called the drafting office of the *Tanganyika Standard* to Government House. A discussion of the statement, line by line, then ensued. The gist of the Governor's criticism, however, was that he considered the statement irresponsible and in making this point he made several disparaging remarks about me as the author. He said that he saw in such a statement, only trouble for Tanganyika, and emphasized that such statements could not benefit Anglo-American relationships.

After my statement was released by the *Tanganyika Standard*, its editor called on the American Counsul-General to discuss it in detail. Using the same line-by-line approach as the Governor, he strongly attacked the validity of the statement's conclusions and indicated that he intended to do a thorough job of editorial surgery on it. He indicated that the statement had brought up all the old criticisms that had been raised against me during the 1954 Visiting Mission. He was particularly disturbed about my assumption that there were present and identifiable TANU leaders who were qualified to assume governmental responsibilities.

The real trouble, of course, lay in the fact that the basic dilemma of the British in East Africa was the recognition of the fact that not one of its territories could advance on its own merits without bringing into play parallel demands of all the adjacent territories. The more rapid advance in government in Tanganyika for example, would have an upsetting effect upon the more slowly developing territories of Kenya, Uganda and Nyasaland. This presented a problem which the British could not resolve to their satisfaction. Indeed, it forced them to violate their clear responsibilities to promote self-government for their Trust Territories as prescribed in the U.N. Charter.

In 1958, shortly after DeGaulle took power in France, the British and French governments agreed to grant combined independence to their Cameroon Trust Territories. This was to take place on January 1, 1960. At first it had appeared to me that a wrong decision had been made, as I had hoped that the British-speaking Cameroons would vote to ally themselves with Nigeria, while the French-speaking Cameroons would assume their own responsibilities. It seemed impractical to me that both territories, speaking different languages, could ever become a lasting entity and I had argued in the past with the leaders of both territories that they should remain apart. In the end, both territories decided to unite for the sole reason that, even though the new nation would be bilingual, both territories were very much opposed to any political ties to the Ibo people of adjacent Nigeria.

The celebration of Cameroon independence took place on January 1, 1960. It was attended by a U.S. delegation headed by Ambassador Lodge, while I was named a Special Ambassador for the occasion. Formal recognition of independence became quite an exciting affair, due to the continued existence of a very active guerrilla opposition known as the Union of Cameroonian People (UPC). The UPC had been calling for earlier independence under the leadership of Reuben Um Nyobé, who had been recently murdered.

Tension between the UPC and the new government was still very high. In fact, the American plane flying the United States Delegation to the festivities arrived at the airport outside of the capital city of Yaounde just a few hours after there had been a guerrilla attack by Nyobé's people on the airport. As a result, when our group debarked, we were escorted to the airport building through a line of Cameroonian soldiers all facing outward with their tommy guns ready to fire on anything that might look suspicious. We were then taken into the city where we were quartered on an empty floor of the Yaounde Hospital, with armed guards constantly patrolling.

During the next few days, there was a series of

receptions, banquets, parades and boat races. The actual independence salute took place officially at 12:00 midnight on the day of our arrival, and was marked by a 101-gun salute.

The next day, the new government organized a huge parade, which wound through streets lined with shouting, but friendly, crowds. The American Delegation was seated not far from where the new President, Ahmadou Ahidjo, was reviewing the celebrating contingents. The parade was headed by several newly formed battalions of Cameroonian troops, who marched splendidly to the martial music of a military band. The soldiers were followed by athletes, boy scouts and girl scouts, and thousands of school children.

From our position during the parade, I had a clear view of President Ahidjo. While watching him on the reviewing stand I kept wondering how long it would be before he would be attacked by the guerrilla organization of Um Nyobé, which was now organized and led by Felix Moumie.

Later on in the day, our delegation visited the house of the American Consul, Mr. Collins, where we were informed that, on the night before, Mr. Collins' cook had been attacked and was seriously wounded by a gang of UPC guerrillas. For some inexplicable reason, these attacks were usually confined to a narrow swath which cut across the city from one end to the other, running like a tornado, destroying all in its path. Why the guerrillas attacked in this fashion has never been explained.

On the following day, the visitors to the celebrations were flown to the coastal city of Douala to review another parade. This one was particularly interesting because one section was composed of UPC forces. It was a large contingent, accompanied by much shouting and singing, with the participants carrying banners calling for the overthrow of the new government. There were many pictures of Um Nyobé, some of which were printed on people's clothing. After the parade at noon, we watched a boat race consisting of large dugout canoes called *pirogues*, which was unusual in that each boat was manned by some 40 paddlers.

The next day, Ambassador Lodge and the other

members of the U.S. Delegation departed for an official visit to Liberia, leaving me to complete our representation in the Cameroons. The celebrations which then took place were outside the large city of Ngoundere, where Ahidjo reviewed most of the Muslim tribal groups which inhabited the interior. This was very interesting because before each delegation passed in review, its particular leader, usually clad in a long white gown and crowned in an enormous colored turban, drove up to the grandstand in his own shiny American-built station wagon and seated himself beside the new President. Following the arrival of each of these dignified men, a large group of his people passed in review singing, dancing and drumming.

In the afternoon, there was a huge reception attended by both British, French and other visiting delegations, as well as hundreds of Cameroonian nationals. My duty on this occasion was to present President Eisenhower's gift to President Ahidjo. After doing this, I left the reception to see what might be taking place in the countryside nearby. I soon came to a village where the people were disbanding from the morning parade and happened to pass by a Cameroonian soldier in the process of removing a chainmail uniform similar to those worn by the Crusaders hundreds of years before. Not far from the village I came upon a large fortress-like structure which was the house of the famous Rei-Bouba, a *lamido* (chief) who had remained autonomous while the French Cameroons were under Colonial Administration.

It is interesting to note that President Ahidjo still survives and has become the leader of one of the longest-standing governments in Africa and, despite the early turmoil and the problems of a bilingual country, the Cameroons has proven to be one of the most peaceful and prosperous of the new African nations.

Second Visiting Mission, 1960, (left to right) P.K. Edmunds - New Zealand, Miguel Lopez - Paraguay, Nyerere, Sears, Omar Loutfi-Egypt

Arrival of Sears Mission in Rwanda/Urundi

Chapter VIII

The 1960 Mission

Following the independence of Cameroon, the Trusteeship Council dispatched a mission to the Trusteeship Territories of Ruanda-Urundi and Tanganyika. Since it was the turn of the United States to head the Mission, I was elected Chairman and was accorded by President Eisenhower the rank of Ambassador. The Mission included P.K. Edmunds of New Zealand, Miguel Solano Lopez of Paraguay, and Ambassador Omar Loutfi of the United Arab Republic. We were also accompanied by well-informed personnel drawn from the U.N. Secretariat.

The Mission first visited Ruanda-Urundi, which was in the midst of tribal warfare and widespread political unrest. It would be difficult to exaggerate the problems and tensions we found in these two territories. In my view, these were due primarily to the belated authorization of a few political rights and a previous refusal to face the implications of growing African nationalism. It was obvious that the Trust Territory of Ruanda-Urundi would ultimately have to be divided between Ruanda on the one hand and Urundi on the other.

We arrived in Ruanda shortly after the death of the Mwami Mutara, who had been the reigning *Mwami* at the time of our 1954 Mission. His death occurred under mysterious circumstances. His death not only came at an inopportune time, it also meant that his strong character and influence would be lacking in his successor. I assumed that the new *Mwami* would have sufficient mystique to hold all the people together—Hutu, Tutsi and Twa. Unfortunately, this was not to be.

My attitude was also influenced by the fact that the Catholic missionaries were pro-Hutu and anti-Tutsi. Yet, on one occasion, I was visited by a group of Protestant missionaries who informed me that a significant political crisis was developing. A few nights before their call upon me, they had seen excited bands of Hutus fanning out from a nearby Catholic church, apparently on their way to pillage and burn Tutsi establishments. Even though I knew that these missionary callers were Protestant and hence likely to be anti-Catholic, I believed their contention. This perception affected my judgment throughout the time the Mission spent in Ruanda-Urundi.

The new *Mwami*, Kigeri, was a man who did not have nearly the strong personal character of his predecessor. Furthermore, although it was agreed that his rule should be based upon constitutional privileges and restrictions, his tenure expired before Ruanda became independent. The uncertainty connected with choosing a new *Mwami* made travel through Ruanda difficult because the people were basically divided between those Tutsi who wished for an immediate independence and the bulk of the Hutu, who wanted delay until elections could be held and they could free themselves from Tutsi domination.

Following the riots in the Congo early in 1959, African nationalism began taking root in Ruanda and Urundi. This was undoubtedly abetted by the late *Mwami* Mutara because of his hostility toward the Belgian Administration. Recognizing the changing political situation, the Government in Brussels dispatched a "working group" to the Territory to draft revised and accelerated plans for the attainment of independence. Mutara's death complicated the situation because it allowed a powerful group of anti-administration leaders in the Tutsi hierarchy to select a new *Mwami* whom they could control. This control became absolutely essential to them after the "working group" published their recommendations for very much accelerated progress of the Territory toward independence.

There were several results from this. One was that the UNAR party had to press harder and harder for immediate independence in order to protect their control of the less-educated Hutu majority. The second was that the Catholic Church became panicky about a possible loss of power to the Mwami and the Tutsi overlords and the probable entrenchment of social injustice to the Hutu, both of which the Church strenuously opposed.

In this situation, the Church acted too hastily by encouraging the organization of an extremely militant movement among the Hutu. This Church-backed movement stimulated the Mwami-Tutsi factionalism, which in turn precipitated the violent pogroms of November, 1959. The massive outbreak of violence caught the Belgian administration off balance and forced it to bring in troops to restore order. To prevent the Church-backed drive for Hutu emancipation from developing into civil war, the Administration decided to support the Hutu drive as long as it remained peaceful.

These actions hardened the positions of both sides. The Administration found itself, with the Church looking over its shoulder, sitting on the side of a dangerously excited anti-UNAR movement among a large section of the Hutu. At the same time, the UNAR leaders and the *Mwami*, with his enormous following among both the Tutsi and the Hutu, was determined to check the opposition and promote their own ideas by putting on bigger and better public demonstrations, especially during our Visiting Mission's presence in the Territory.

The UNAR movement derived its strength from two sources. One was the institution of the *Mwami* and its "mystique," which still retained a considerable following among the Hutu. The other came from UNAR association with the African nationalist and independence movements all over Africa.

The UNAR drive for immediate independence was buttressed by the independence which had come to the Congo in

June and also by the rapid progress being made toward independence in Tanganyika. At the time, it seemed to me that the Belgian Administration could count on no more than two years, possibly even less, within which to prepare the Territory for the end of its Trusteeship. African leaders on both sides used intimidation and false rumors to play upon the fears of their largely Hutu followers and any disorderly incidents between the political parties would almost guarantee the outbreak of further violence.

The Mission traveled the length and breadth of the Territory and was greeted by literally thousands and thousands of Ruandans who were most anxious to have our Mission well-informed about their point of view. What made our excursions truly dramatic was the fact that the competing factions were usually lined up on either side of the roads along which we traveled. Whereas the 1954 Visiting Mission had received practically no petitions, the opposing parties of Ruandans in 1960 continuously filled our cars with petitions expressing their wishes. It is no exaggeration to say that many thousands of people lined the roads. In looking back, it still seems extraordinary that we never saw these crowds attack one another although we were informed that on some occasions there was violence and even killing after we had departed.

During its stay in Ruanda, the Mission held numerous and well-attended meetings during which we attempted to devise a system of self-government to which all Ruandan factions could agree. In the end, the Tutsi did not prevail and the Hutu majority succeeded in replacing the new *Mwami* with a democratically-elected Hutu President, Kayibanda.

In Urundi, now called Burundi, the political conditions were much less turbulent. The *Mwami*, Mwanbutsa, enjoyed a European life style and was well-known as a playboy. He exhibited less interest in the political advancement of his people than had the more politically-oriented Mwami Mutara of Ruanda.

Our final days in the Belgian Trust Territories were spent in Urundi in the city of Usumbura (now Bujumbura), where there was great concern over the political disturbances which were taking place in the countryside. The situation here differed from the

Tutsi-Hutu dispute in Ruanda in that it was a struggle between the royal princes on the one side and both Tutsis and Hutus on the other. The latter side was led by Chief Baranyanka and his sons and Joe Baroli, their organizer.

Baroli explained that the ruling Tutsis under the *Mwami* used the Batwa pigmies as their fighters, but that the traditional UPRONA party employed the Swahili-speaking Africans who came from Tanganyika to do their dirty work. He said his car had been stoned by the Swahilis and that, unless something dramatic was accomplished, there would be serious violence in Urundi. I felt sad when I said good-bye to Baroli for he had told me that he was very much disturbed about his political future, and that he felt obliged to carry a gun at all times. His sense of danger proved all too well-founded, for he was murdered a year or two later.

The final breakup of the double Trust Territory took place in 1961, when Rwagasore, the son of Mwami Mwambutsa, won the elections in Urundi, defeating Baroli and his party. Rwagasore's party won 58 of the 64 seats in the legislature and he became the first Prime Minister of Mwami Mwambutsa, who continued on his throne as a constitutional monarch.

In Ruanda, the Parmehutu party, led by Kayibanda, won 35 of the 44 seats, while the *Mwami's* party, the UNAR, won only 7 seats. Rwagasana was elected in a vote which rejected the institution of *Mwami* by a four-to-one margin. Independence on the basis of two separate nations was formalized in 1962.

After our stay in Usumbura, we flew to Dar es Salaam, the capital of Tanganyika, where political progress was developing in a satisfactory manner. We were met at the airport by Mr. Fletcher-Cook, who was Secretary of the Territory and next in rank to the Governor. Fletcher-Cook had frequently attended sessions of the Trusteeship Council as Special Representative to report to the Council on conditions in Tanganyika.

On the evening of our arrival the Governor, Sir Richard Turnbull, gave a large reception for the Mission. During this affair he invited me to accompany him on a sunrise bicycle ride through the streets of Dar es Salaam on the following morning. I told him I would be delighted to accept and then proceeded to check with other people as to whether or not the Governor meant what he said. I was informed that it was a serious invitation. This put me on my mettle because, even though I had not ridden a bicycle for over 40 years, I did not intend to let any British official get the better of me! The bicycle trip was scheduled to begin at 5 o'clock the next morning, at which time the Governor appeared at my hotel with his aide and an extra bicycle. They were also accompanied by the African Mayor of Dar es Salaam and the leading Indian businessman. After some initial difficulties, I was able to span the 40 years of inexperience and was able to pedal along satisfactorily. While our small bicycle procession, led by the Governor, went along in single file, the city of Dar es Salaam was preparing for a new day.

A few days after the Mission's arrival, I attended a meeting at the house of U.S. Consul-General Duggan, also attended by Julius Nyerere. The purpose of the meeting was to discuss with Nyerere the various ways the United States could assist him in promoting the political progress which had already begun in the Trust Territory. Without our knowledge, the British police had placed a secret listening device in the room where we were talking.

As these meetings were confidential, I had no hesitancy in taking part in such a discussion. Also, most African leaders knew that I had not been supported by the State Department and realized that I represented the prevailing American point of view with respect to carrying out the anti-colonial provisions of the U.N. Charter.

In retrospect, I must admit that I had become so encouraged by the political progress which was taking place that I did not hesitate to express my feelings about the approach of independence. This, of course, did not sit well among the British residents and officials, but it served my purpose and my belief that although I did not enjoy the support of the European division of the American State Department, I did represent the popular sentiments of most Americans on the colonial issue.

Perhaps I was too outspoken, but most of my comments had been made in private conversations. I was subsequently taken aback when, upon our return to Dar es Salaam, I was immediately visited by a young Consul from the U.S. Consulate-General, who informed me that the British government had become disturbed and had complained to Ambassador Whitney in London that I had been too outspoken about political progress in Tanganyika. Actually, this did not cause me any subsequent difficulties because, by this time, Christian Herter had succeeded Mr. Dulles as Secretary of State and he was not as tied to the views of the European Division of the State Department as Mr. Dulles. Soon, however, Secretary Herter was sufficiently interested and sympathetic to my efforts to request that all dispatches concerned with my activities be placed on his desk.

The whole episode concerned me enough that I called on Fletcher-Cook and told him that such treatment of the Chairman of a Visiting Mission was unacceptable and that I wanted an official apology. In the meantime, I made as many public speeches as possible in an endeavor to reassure the British and the Indians that our Mission had only complimentary thoughts about their work and their situation in the Trust Territory.

During our travels we visited the famous Chagga tribe, who lived on the slopes of Mt. Kilimanjaro and had made a large profit out of coffee. A year or two after our visit to the Chagga, the tribe dismissed its traditional chief because he had acted too much like a British official.

In reporting the usually rather uninteresting duties which are normally demanded of a Visiting Mission, there were two events which are worth describing. The first was that one morning while I was conferring with Consul-General Duggan, cables began to come in concerning the Sharpeville Massacre in South Africa. This was a shocking affair, the details of which were carried by the Press all over the world.

The inhuman South African pass laws mobilized several thousand nonviolent protestors who were fired on by the South African police and 80 Africans were killed. The facts surrounding the Sharpeville Massacre have remained for many years a bitter reminder to the white South Africans of what can happen if the Black Africans are pressed too hard by their white rulers.

The second adventure concerned the operations of the British government in preventing the outbreak of a violent cattle war between the Masai tribe on the Serengeti Plain and the Sukuma people who live on the shores of Lake Victoria. It appeared that the Sukuma had crossed 100 miles of the Serengeti Plain and had stolen hundreds of Masai cattle. Among other things, it illustrated the value which many African societies place upon the possession of cattle, for these are used as a medium of exchange, a "savings account," and are all-important in terms of paying the "bride price."

My contact with the cattle raid occurred around Game Park Lodge at Seronera in the center of the Serengeti Plain, where British Provincial and District commissioners and police officials were trying to prevent a war between a regiment of 500 or more Masai Moran and a group of Sukuma. The trouble had arisen over the Sukuma theft of hundreds of cattle from the Masai elders deep in the interior of the Serengeti. Upon my arrival at Seronera, it was not yet known which particular Sukuma group had stolen the cattle, exactly where the bulk of the Masai Moran were headed, or where the cattle had been taken. When I arrived, very considerable police forces, in cars equipped with radios, had been gradually closing in on the Masai warriors.

I came to Seronera in a tiny plane which had been chartered by the government to help scout for the Masai and to transport officials in and out of the Serengeti.

It was an unforgettable flight from the town of Arusha, which is a sort of northern diplomatic capital for Tanganyika. The plane was so small and was loaded with so much luggage for use at Seronera that there was no place to store my briefcase, which was all that I was carrying. Because of the lack of space I was obliged to hold my briefcase on my lap while my knees were tightly wedged against the instrument panel of the plane. Since the plane was very slow and old-fashioned, the flight lasted two hours, yet it was an exciting ride. We flew past one side of the mountains ringing the Ngorongoro Crater to reach the tremendous expanse of the Serengeti, stretching off into the distant horizon. The plain appeared to be treeless, just one stretch of very green meadow, like a huge lawn on which there were thousands and thousands of zebra, wildebeest (gnus) and gazelle. We saw one rhino cantering along while we made a wide circle above him. One herd of wildebeest must have numbered thirty or forty thousand animals.

Finally, we got to the grass landing strip at the Seronera camp to find that two other planes had also just landed there, one flying in with Provincial Commissioner Harris of the Lake Province. It was from this province that the Sukuma traveled into the Masai area where they stole the Masai cattle. The British immediately began dispatching motorized police onto the plains and managed to get to the Masai, persuading them to halt for a while so that the British had a chance to determine which group had carried out the cattle raid. More police units had been ordered to close in on the Masai from different directions. Shortly after our plane landed, two carloads of people arrived. They included the District Commissioner of Masailand, Francis Townsend (brother of Peter Townsend, who Princess Margaret wanted to marry at one time), and three of the leaders of the Masai Moran and the two elders from whom the cattle had been stolen. The Moran had their forelocks pulled down over their foreheads and tightened by a clasp. This, I was told, indicated that they were ready for battle and were prepared to die. There followed a long discussion which was subsequently translated to me. It appeared that the British were still very much in the dark as to where the bulk of the Masai had moved. Francis Townsend had failed to find where they had gone, but acting on a tip, decided to move on to a place where it was hoped they could be located.

The next day I had breakfast with Mr. and Mrs. Harvey, the Park Wardens. During the meal, they used a supply of moths which they had caught the night before to attract flycatchers. These small birds fluttered down and snatched the moths from their fingers—even once from mine. Then we went outside to feed a huge cockroach to a lizard—a rather large one—who expected to be fed. He was in his usual place on the side of the house waiting. Mr. Harvey placed the cockroach on a ledge below him and the lizard immediately started down for it, got quite close, and stopped for a second—just enough to allow a small flycatcher to dash in and seize the insect from right under the lizard's jaws.

After breakfast I went to a group of small thatched huts (called *rondavels*) where the police and the administration officials were discussing the latest news about the impending events, which might provoke a battle between the Masai Moran and the Sukuma.

Word had come during the night that the main contingent of Masai, who had previously agreed to a British request to remain stationary for a day or two until the British could locate their stolen cattle and return them, had found fresh cattle tracks and had instantly started off to get their cattle back. The British District Commissioners who had conferred with the Moran told me that they were in a very angry mood, and had gotten so excited that they jumped up and down. One of the District Commissioners said he feared some of these Moran might attack him personally in their excitement.

In the meantime, another plane came in to Seronera, reporting that the Sukuma men were mobilizing and moving out to meet the Masai. There followed a long but unsuccessful effort by the police to make radio contact with a communication point nearest to the locality where the clash was most likely to occur. The police wanted to get the information across to Provincial Commissioner Harris that District Commissioner Townsend was on his way to where the Masai were and should be there in two hours. Townsend had great influence with the Masai and it was hoped that he could calm them down, avoiding bloodshed.

While all this was going on, another complication arose due to the failure of an airplane to arrive carrying valuable information about the overall situation. When the plane finally arrived, the two police officials who got out had a marvelous story to tell. The plane had actually located the Masai strung out in a long attack line with each Moran squatting behind his shield, while hundreds of Sukuma, with their faces covered with white war paint, were jumping up and down as they approached the Masai line.

Behind the developing battle lines Sukuma from all over were rushing up to join the fight. Some of the Masai wore lion headdress and all were covered with red ochre mud. The Sukuma actually got within one hundred yards of the Masai while four very brave African policemen stood between the two advancing lines, trying frantically to get them to halt their attack.

It was at this point that the plane carrying the police arrived, just in time for them to dive down in front of the advancing lines in an attempt to frighten them back and delay a clash. I asked if they flew as low as twenty feet and they said much lower. This buzzing, repeated several times, had the effect of delaying the attack. A detachment of motorized police and several British officials arrived at that moment and succeeded in stopping further developments. Both the Sukuma and the Masai fight with bows and poisoned arrows to begin with, and then use knives as they close in, if one side by that time had not decided to flee. The Sukuma poison, however, is more deadly than the Masai's, and is said to kill within twenty minutes. If they had actually started shooting, these four brave policemen in between them would surely have been killed. Another thing that interested me was that when the Sukuma got into a fight they cover their faces with white paint and sometimes wear feathers. Normally, these Africans would be wearing European shorts and shirts. After this crisis had been averted, I decided to return to Musoma, where I was due to rejoin the Mission.

The work of the Visiting Mission having been completed in Tanganyika, we made preparations to depart from Dar es Salaam for London. We were very surprised to find that Governor Sir Richard Turnbull was present at the airport to wish the Mission good-bye. As this was a most unusual break in custom, his surprising attendance indicated that my complaints to Fletcher-Cook concerning our less-than-courteous reception had borne results.

To carry the matter still further, the day after our arrival in London, the Mission assembled in an anteroom outside of the office of the Colonial Secretary, Mr. Ian MacLeod, to report our findings to him. While we were waiting to go into his office, a messenger requested me to meet with the Colonial Secretary ahead of other Mission members. Upon entering his office, I found Mr. MacLeod and Lord Perth, the Minister of State for Colonial Affairs, waiting to apologize to me for the treatment which I, as Chairman of the Mission, had received on certain occasions during our travels through Tanganyika. I responded to them that it had been very annoying. The Secretary and Lord Perth replied that it had also been most annoying to them. In fact, they were so decent to me that I told them that when two gentlemen such as they could be so understanding, I could do nothing but state how much I appreciated their attitude and would forget the whole matter.

Subsequently, the other members of the Mission joined me so that we could render the nature of our report on the Trust Territory. Both the Secretary and Lord Perth observed that they were delighted by our observations and soon hoped to make Tanganyika a prize example of their Territorial Trust operations.

After the chastizing which I had received following the report of the 1954 Visiting Mission, their comments about our visit were more than appreciated and provided a very happy ending to the 1960 Visiting Mission.

Second Sears Mission to Tanzania

Chapter IX

Deluge of Independence

On the western side of the continent, the year 1960 brought a deluge of independence. With the exception of Portugal, it broke the back of the European empires in Africa. In total, fifteen new nations became independent. Of this number, thirteen were French, and the remaining two were Nigeria and the former Belgian Congo. Nigeria became the largest and most important Black government in Africa, while the Congo broke apart before its independence was several weeks old.

Early in January, 1959, I wrote a report concerning U.S. relationships with African nationalism for Ambassador Lodge. The phenomenal growth of African nationalism in the late 1950's and the U.S. opposition to it had become a source of great concern to me. Therefore, I submitted the following memorandum to Ambassador Lodge, believing that he would agree with its contents and transmit it to Secretary of State Herter.

It is not difficult to see what the advent of African independence means for Kenya, where whites and blacks are deadlocked over African demands for more political rights. But the question here is not what the Government has done or intends to do, but what Tom

Mboya and his associate, Dr. Kiano, decide to do about it. They hold the initiative as nationalist leaders so often do, and what they decide will make the history of Kenya tomorrow. These leaders have recently warned that unless the Kenya Government grants universal suffrage, the Africans would boycott elections, and refuse to buy in white shops or work for white settlers. At that point Kenya would be close to civil disobedience and violence.

Another very critical situation is developing in British Central Africa where the Federation of the two Rhodesias and Nyasaland is headed for a breakup instead of independence. But here again, as in Kenya, the history of tomorrow will be written more by African leaders than by Sir Roy Welensky, the Federal Prime Minister. Welensky's hands are tied by a European electorate, of some 250,000 people living mostly in Southern Rhodesia, which is a territory almost as segregation minded as the Union of South Africa. At the pace Africa is going today, it would be completely unrealistic to believe that these Europeans will be able or willing to change their lifelong ways of white supremacy in time to dissuade the African majorities of the Northern Rhodesian and Nyasaland protectorates from forcing their way out of the European controlled Federation.

The key opponent to federation is Dr. Banda, a fanatic on independence for Nyasaland. I had three talks with him and was much impressed by the emotional quality of his ambition which, for the moment, is utterly unconcerned over the inability of Nyasaland to support itself much above a subsistence level after independence. But Dr. Banda is almost a Messiah to the Nyasa people, and has played upon their mass excitability so successfully that anti-white violence has already begun and my guess is that it will almost certainly get worse until Dr. Banda is eventually arrested and put away. The situation is really serious and British officials told me they see little hope of keeping Nyasaland in the Federation. If Nyasaland breaks away, Northern Rhodesia will follow. Politically it will have no other choice.

Meanwhile Southern Rhodesia under its European rule is mesmerized by its politicians and dreams on about Federal independence. There is no sense of urgency about advancing its own Africans politically, and no sensitivity at all about the hostility it has incurred among the Africans in the two northern protectorates whose approval is necessary for final independence. But when it does wake up and finds that Parliament in London is unwilling to force a new white supremacy nation of Africa, it may create such bad blood between the Rhodesian settlers and the British Government that Southern Rhodesia may be tempted to join the Union of South Africa, regardless of the rebellion it might precipitate among its 2,500,000 Africans.

A situation which is even more serious than in British Central Africa has arisen in the Congo where there has been rioting and bloodshed in the one large territory where the standard of living of urban Africans is better than anywhere else in the continent. The trouble there is that past Belgian suppression of everything political has left the territory in a political vacuum, with no well defined organization under African leadership—like the African National Congresses of other territories—which has the ear of more than a limited number of people. Political reform, under these circumstances, may be difficult to set in motion, because there will be too many aspiring politicians, all of them anxious to get into the act. But since few of them can be accepted as leaders in the beginning, it may mean considerably more rioting before the situation becomes stabilized. Even if this is happily not the case the example of the political awakening of the Congo will have a very contagious influence on the growing unrest in other parts of Africa. Furthermore, the fact that the initial rioting in Leopoldville was quickly followed by a proclamation— actually in preparation before the riots—that Belgium would lead the Congo to ultimate independence, will now be twisted by African extremists to prove that the only road to political emancipation is through violence.

All of these situations—from Kenya, to the Rhodesias, to the Congo, not to mention South Africa— are building up at approximately the same time, and will probably interact one upon another, under the coordinating influence of the recent All African People's Conference.

At this point I would like to speculate for a

moment on the dilemma which now confronts the Colonial Governments, because it has a bearing on the pace of development of the Trust Territories of Tanganyika and possibly Ruanda-Urundi.

What most of the Nationalist leaders will be demanding immediately is universal suffrage which is already in operation throughout British West Africa and in all French Territories, including French Equatorial Africa. It will also be granted to the Congolese this year. If it has become an accepted institution in so many places, it can be equally accepted in the rest of Africa—according to African reasoning which would be hard to refute. But if universal suffrage is granted to East and Central Africa and the Congo, it would not be more than a matter of months, or a year or two at best, before the Africans would gain complete political control of their respective territories. After that they would be in a bargaining position and could do what they liked on independence, which would be intolerable to the settler communities.

This leaves the British Government, in particular, in a fix. If they do not give universal suffrage to their remaining territories at once—and if they give it to one they might then have to give it to all—there is certain to be organized violence against them by the Africans. On the other hand, if they do grant it now, the European communities—perhaps literally—will be up in arms. Thus in one way or another an African crisis is around the corner, and its prospects will not be minimized by the mass emergence of new African nations next year.

In any case the moment is near when the Soviet Union will be given its greatest opportunity to split the world in two, by gaining a controlling influence over Africa through its Nationalist movements. Secretary Dulles has frequently warned about this. But there is no reason why the U.S. should not also compete for Nationalist goodwill. The recommendations which follow will suggest how the U.S. can ride along with the Nationalist bandwagon without actually climbing on board, or without taking sides against its European allies.

These proposals may seem inadequate to meet the serious situation arising in Africa but they are only meant to meet the particular point which African

Nationalism raises at this moment.
Here are the recommendations:

*Recommendation 1 - The State
Department should encourage U.S. Embassies and
Consulates to increase the number and the frequency of
their contacts with Nationalist leaders.* The importance
of this could be far reaching for the U.S. Seldom have so
many new states been coming to life at the same time, on
the same continent, under the leadership of so few people.
Because there is a scarcity as yet of experienced African
leaders, it is easy to identify and to build goodwill among
the actual individuals who are about to become the Prime
Ministers, and the other prominent citizens of their
respective countries. The establishment of friendly
contacts with these leaders should be one of the principle
duties of those who represent the U.S. in Africa. Such
meetings should be for the important purposes of keeping
up with African thinking and making friends for the U.S.
There can be no valid objections to this by the Colonial
authorities. Nevertheless, there may be a reluctance
among some of our representatives to undertake this kind
of activity, unless they are periodically prodded by the
State Department.

*Recommendation 2 - The State
Department should dispatch a representative to Africa
periodically for the particular purpose of calling upon
various African leaders.* This would give on the spot
emphasis to the State Department's direct interest in
Nationalist thinking, which would be much appreciated
by the Africans. It would also put regularity into the
contact procedure and make it easier for the Consulates
to expand their contacts. Having recently called upon
many of the leading Nationalists in East and Central
Africa, I can report that this approach to the Nationalist
movement contains a gold mine of goodwill for the U.S.

*Recommendation 3 - Congress should be
requested to make additional appropriations for leader
grants so that a much larger number of African political
leaders may be invited to the U.S.* This would be one of
the cheapest and most effective ways to build goodwill.
For less than one half the cost of one U.S. Sabre Jet, a
large cross section of African political leaders could be

invited for a short visit to the U.S., provided with suitable travel escorts, and returned to Africa with some understanding of American life. Under present appropriations it has not been possible to invite more than a handful of political leaders. Few if any of the Prime Ministers in the 12 Locally Autonomous Republics or territories of French West and Equatorial Africa have ever set foot in the U.S., although most of them have visited Paris. Likewise, very few African leaders from the Congo or from the Rhodesias or Nyasaland have visited this country. An expanded U.S. program for African political visitors would compete effectively with the open house program which the Soviet Union and its satellites maintain for African visitors.

Recommendation 4 - More forthright statements should be made by the U.S. Representatives in the U.N. which would unmistakably throw U.S. moral support behind legitimate Nationalist aspirations. During the 1958 session of the General Assembly, the U.S. made some very helpful moves toward a pro-African position on Algerian independence and on the South African race issue. It is hoped that these were only first steps which will be followed by further equally helpful steps in the next General Assembly. Because of the intense importance which Africans everywhere attach to these issues, the position of the U.S. on them has a vital bearing on American prestige from one end of the continent to the other.

The U.S. has so many critically urgent problems in Europe and Asia that one hesitates to emphasize others. But I believe that a dangerous crisis in Africa is so close at hand that there is no time to lose any opportunity, however small, to build goodwill among those who will be leading the independent Africa of tomorrow.

Following my submission of this memorandum, Ambassador Lodge and I obtained the approval of Secretary of State Herter for a conference of United States representatives on duty in Africa. From it, we hoped would come positive action to get U.S.-

African policy moving in the right direction. The conference was held in Lorenço Marques, capital of Mozambique, and as anticipated, produced almost unanimous backing for the development of closer and more sympathetic personal contacts with African nationalist leaders. Unhappily, our Ambassador to the Union of South Africa opposed the idea. He seemed oblivious to the continental-wide danger which might one day pit the five million white-supremacy-minded whites of Africa against the more than 200 million blacks. Such a situation could easily threaten international peace and make southern Africa a flash point.

Unfortunately, the conference ultimately turned out to be a waste of time. Bureaucratic inertia in the State Department was partly to blame, but there is little doubt that considerable opposition came from the State Department's influential European Division. The foreign service officers of this division were opposed to any support for African nationalist causes, believing them to be offensive to our NATO allies. These officers seemed out of touch with the realities of the situation. In fact, less than one year later, the deluge came. Given a choice between remaining a part of the French Union, local autonomy, or complete independence of a kind which would qualify them for membership in the U.N., the Africans voted for complete independence. It was surprising that the often-astute French failed to appreciate the prestige of independence and the appeal of freedom.

After World War II, French government policy did its best to organize its African colonies so that each colony became a full-fledged province of France. This referendum ended the French empire. French relationships in Africa were transformed into what came to be known as the French Community. This was similar to the policy that the British had developed in their largely successful efforts to construct a truly international Commonwealth.

After the 1959 referendum, the French lost no time in liquidating their African empire, and in less than a year, there remained only a single French outpost at Djibouti. However, there were those who felt that the French had proceeded with undue haste. For example, Ambassador Robert Murphy, U.S. Representative at the independence celebrations of the Belgian Congo, was one of the more eloquent of these. During his stay in Leopoldville, capital of the newly-independent Congo, Murphy visited Brazzaville, capital of the former French Congo, which had been independent for several months. In his memoirs, *Diplomat Among Warriors*, Murphy recalls his impressions of Congo-Brazzaville. He became convinced that the French policy was mistaken, not only in the Congo, but throughout its colonies in West Africa. In his view, a mature sense of political reality was absent from French policy for it seemed to do nothing more than guarantee that the Africans would not be ready for responsible self-government when independence came. Violence seemed, to him, certain to occur in the former French Congo.

In contrast to this, Murphy felt that there would be no outbreak of violence in the Belgian Congo, where the paternalistic attitude of the Belgians in seeking economic rather than political development would insure responsible self-government. He then returned to Washington only to learn that shortly after his visit the newly-launched Congolese state had been completely shattered and that the Belgians were fleeing for their lives. To a man of his great experience and diplomatic skills, it must have been disconcerting to realize that he had so misjudged the situation in the Congo. It is a pity that the unsympathetic U.S. foreign policy towards the reality of spreading African nationalism had misfired. Perhaps little more could be expected from one who had been an architect of that policy.

In December, 1961, I was invited to attend the independence ceremonies of Tanganyika at Dar es Salaam. From my standpoint, this was a very gratifying occasion. I could not help but remember the heated British criticism of my role as a member of the 1954 Visiting Mission, during which I threw U.S. support to the claim that Tanganyikan independence could be achieved as early as 1974. That independence came within seven years instead of the twenty years originally contemplated, making the celebrations a very significant reflection of the failure of many white people to give due recognition to the impact of nationalism upon colonial Africa.

An interesting feature of the various activities which my wife and I were privileged to attend was the presence of Jomo

Kenyatta at the side of Prime Minister Nyerere at most of the celebration activities. Kenyatta had only recently been released from his exile at Lodwar on the northern frontier of Kenya.

On the night that independence actually went into effect, the British Union Jack was lowered and the green, yellow, blue and black flag of Tanzania was raised to the masthead. The stadium, which had been built especially for the occasion, was filling up not only with thousands of Africans, but also with a very large number of British officials. It being a full-dress affair, the British guests were clad in tuxedos or white ties and tail coats. While my wife and I were watching this gathering of somberly dressed British officials, our attention was suddenly drawn to a flash of color which turned out to be Jomo Kenyatta, clad in leopard skins instead of his usual European dress. To see this single individual walking slowly to his seat dressed in defiance of the white man's customs had a telling effect upon everybody, since it served as a reminder that Kenya itself would soon become free.

Hatred of Kenyatta was rampant among most of the British, who still blamed him for the Mau Mau atrocities. On one occasion, when a large garden party was being held, Ralph Bunche, the distinguished American Under Secretary-General of the U.N., introduced my wife and I to Kenyatta. At the time, my wife had been taking tea with a group of English ladies. After meeting Kenyatta, she returned to the group only to find that these ladies were very much upset that she had shaken hands with such a hateful man.

Governor Sir Richard Turnbull had become very friendly towards me. This was extremely pleasant, considering the feelings he had expressed against me after my speech in the Trusteeship Council warning that conditions in a slowly-developing Kenya should not delay the progress toward independence which the Trust Territory of Tanganyika was already enjoying.

On the final evening of the celebrations, Prime Minister Nyerere held one of those famous British-style receptions, in which attending royalty is customarily introduced to those guests lucky enough to be selected for the privilege. On this occasion, the reception was crowded with a great many British people, who lined an open lane so that the guest of honor, Prince Philip, might walk through, in order to be introduced to the lucky ones by Prime Minister Nyerere. It being a British affair, my wife and I decided it was appropriate to retire from a front-row position to a spot well back and relatively hidden among the British guests. At the appointed moment, as Nyerere began to lead the Prince among the crowd, I was somewhat taken aback when Nyerere pointed toward me, indicating that he wanted my wife and I to come forward so that we could be the first to be introduced to the Prince. In response we moved to the front of the crowd in order to shake hands with the Prime Minister and Prince Philip. The Prince asked me about my interest in Tanganyika and I told him that I was practically a member of TANU inasmuch as I had so strongly backed Tanganyika for its early independence!

On the last day of the celebrations, at a final lawn party, I found Prime Minister Nyerere and my friend Sylvanus Olympio, the Prime Minister of Togo, strolling together, apart from the crowd. This gave me an opportunity to join the two men so that I could thank Prime Minister Nyerere for inviting my wife and I to tne celebrations. As he and Olympio turned to see me, they remarked that my approach was a coincidence as they had been discussing the early arrival of independence following the contentious report of the 1954 Visiting Mission. Sadly, a few weeks later, Sylvanus Olympio was murdered near his home in Togo.

One of the things that stands out most clearly in my mind when recalling the Tanganyika independence celebrations was the statement made by Julius Nyerere that, "the people of Tanganyika would like to light a candle and put it on the top of Mt. Kilimanjaro [so that it could] shine beyond our borders as a ray of hope to all our fellow men, wherever they may be."

As an aftermath of the sweep of independence over all but the southern end of Africa, there was considerable political confusion and unrest. The result was that many of the newly independent governments were overthrown by military personnel. As a result, there were many people who questioned whether African independence may have been prematurely won. The question, however, is not relevant since independence came when it had to come, and it had to come before violence spread all over the continent. The troublesome periods which have accompanied the first years of independence contained nothing particularly new historically, and may be compared with similar periods which have occurred during the birth of non-African nations in every quarter of the world. It is worthwhile to keep in mind the speed and safe manner in which the new African nations have been able to exchange their status as colonies for a new life of independence.

Important analyses pertaining to the evolutions of nations are packed with the stories of political progress which at one time or another became dangerously violent and even revolutionary. In Japan, for example, the absolute power of the ancient line of emperors was displaced for a time in the not too distant past by the fierce Samurai warriors of the Shogunate. And though less spectacular, the orderly progress of government in Japan continues to this day to be handicapped by the unrestrained anti-government rioting of thousands of discontented students—a state of affairs common in many other countries.

The record of battle-scarred Europe has been one of ever-changing frontiers brought on by war after war and the intemperate attitude of belligerent leaders such as Napoleon, Kaiser Wilhelm and Stalin. It has been said, with some validity, that the history of the world, from the Crusaders on through World War II, shows that Europe contains the most warlike people on the face of the earth.

The politics of Latin America with its endless local revolutions, has become a sickness of endemic proportions. Hopefully, it will not be too long before these revolutions have become a thing of the past.

The United States, itself, has had its share of troubles. These have accompanied, and continue to accompany, the normal running of its government. In spite of this, the U.S. has earned the distinction of being the oldest republic in the world. This has come about because of the nature of conditions in Europe where kingdoms and short-lived republics have been swinging back and forth. In short, the U.S. did not get where it is today without many trials and tribulations. For example, a few years after the American Revolution, Congress reversed its initial republican idealism by authorizing the infamous Alien and Sedition Acts. These acts created a set of very repressive laws under which citizens were exposed to severe punishments if they were accused of what some arbitrary committee considered to be anti-American activities. Aliens similarly charged were deported forthwith. Had these acts remained unrepealed, the United States might have become more authoritarian. Fortunately, however, the inheritance of the American Revolution and the brilliant philosophies worked out by the founding fathers insured that popular opinion would not permit these acts to remain on the books.

The American Civil War was also a tragic period involving a loss of life greater than had yet occurred in the history of modern warfare. The Civil War was followed by Reconstruction, a period unworthy of the American dream.

Turning back to Africa and its tribal complexities, during the Berlin Conference of 1885, competition between the European powers for the development of colonial empires led them to arbitrarily, and without thought for African welfare, divide Africa into spheres of influence with highly arbitrary frontiers. Among nearly all African leaders, it is now openly admitted, however, that a new continent, divided up along ethnic lines, would be an area so Balkanized that these new states would be too weak to function effectively.

Another aspect of the decolonization of Africa concerns the now generally recognized ability of what was heretofore considered "primitive" Africans, to undertake the governmental processes necessary to run a modern nation.

It should be remembered that the time between the beginning of the colonial era and the attainment of independence for most African nations has been quite brief. The changeover of African life from purely tribal restrictions to a consciousness of national life is taking place at a pace which has equalled, and sometimes exceeded, the rate of progress achieved in similar situations in other parts of the world. It is true that large numbers of Africans have not yet wrenched themselves loose from subsistence living. But the noteworthy fact is that so many people have already achieved a higher standard of living than they had enjoyed previously. Again, this compares favorably with the record of non-African peoples to undertake their own forms of self-government.

With most of Africa having won its independence, the question becomes: how long will it be possible for the white-supremacist minorities of southern Africa to hold the line? Most interested observers abroad, as well as in Africa, believe that southern Africa, including Zimbabwe (Rhodesia), Namibia (South-West Africa) and the Republic of South Africa, is a veritable powder keg which could blow up at any time.

In spite of these explosive situations, the white minorities, particularly those in Rhodesia and South Africa, believe they can maintain their rule over millions of Black Africans. How long this can last remains a fair question. The British could not hold on in Asia. The French were unable to overcome the Algerians' drive for independence and were defeated in Indo-China. Both these countries were forced to relinquish their colonies in Africa. The United States could not conquer the Vietnamese. There is a lesson here which must be kept in mind. Military operations against overseas peoples cannot be carried out successfully if there is widespread opposition to them in the areas where the fighting is taking place. The successful waging of overseas military operations becomes impossible if the people at home are unsympathetic with the war effort.

Past records show some of the specific reasons why this is so. In Great Britain, for example, it is impossible to conceive that there could have been any attempt to prevent, by force of arms, the demands for independence made by India, especially after World War II, during which India contributed several million soldiers to the survival of Britain itself. It is obvious that the winning of independence by India led the way for the subsequent downfall of colonialism throughout most of the world. When Britain lost India, it began to lose its colonial empire. Its prestige was saved by the transformation of the Empire into a commonwealth of freely-associated nations.

In the case of France, the unsuccessful use of 400,000 troops in Algeria spoke eloquently of the failure of even huge modern military forces to subdue determined resistance by guerrilla freedom fighters aided by the local populace.

More than anything else, however, it has been the dismal record of the United States in its prosecution of the Vietnam War that clearly illustrates the shocking military miscalculations which marked the U.S. failure to crush the Vietnamese people. From the beginning, the military misjudgments made by the U.S. were considerable. The most spectacular was the absurd assumption that unrestricted air warfare would destroy the power and determination of the North Vietnamese people to resist. To understand the depth of the U.S. miscalculations one has only to reflect upon the effect of the massive German bombing of Great Britain during World War II. The resistance of the British populace during the Battle of Britain has become legendary, and the assumption that the Vietnamese would not exhibit the same type of resistance was totally unfounded. Eventually, the tonnage of bombs dropped on Vietnam exceeded that dropped during World War II. All this was done to a country of the size of the state of Arizona.

More than any other example, the American failure in Vietnam has shown that it is impossible for a large and powerful country to undermine the ability of a small nation to determine its own future. It also has demonstrated that such an attempt by a large nation can have disastrous effects upon the internal political processes of that nation itself, as when Lyndon Johnson was hounded from office due to the unpopularity of the Vietnam War. History will undoubtedly expose the white supremacists in southern Africa to the same fate that France, Great Britain and the United States enjoyed in their attempts to subjugate developing peoples. This aftermath of African independence seems inevitable to me.

Chapter X

African Independence and Its Implications for United States Policy

Any review of American policy toward Africa during the 1950's and the early 1960's cannot help but reveal a widespread lack of understanding of the importance of African nationalism. There was, however, one satisfactory discussion of American policy that aligned us with every country represented in the U.N. except Great Britain, France, Australia and Portugal. This was the position we took on the question of South-West Africa (Namibia). While Great Britain, France, Portugal and Australia could be regularly counted upon to vote with South Africa, the rest of the U.N., including the U.S., voted the other way.

Most countries argued that the U.N. was the successor organization to the League of Nations and that, legally speaking, a mandated territory under the League was, in fact, a Trust Territory under the U.N. Charter. As we have seen, this was so in the case of the Trust Territories of both British and French Cameroon, British and French Togoland, Belgian Ruanda-Urundi, and Tanganyika. South Africa, however, did not agree that these cases applied to them. It was adamant on the subject and for a long time refused even to discuss the question. The official attitude of the U.S. toward this *impasse* was that, with a little patience, South Africa might yet be persuaded to participate in a conference which could result in a

149

solution acceptable to both sides.

When South Africa rejected this conciliatory proposal, the only two African nations which had been members of the League, Ethiopia and Liberia, represented the League in requesting the International Court of Justice to rule whether or not South-West Africa was an integral part of South Africa or a U.N. Trust Territory. Unhappily, the Court refused to rule on the grounds that Liberia and Ethiopia did not have proper standing. The procedure of the Court in rejecting the request reflected an unconscionable and ethically unsupportable action by the Australian president of the Court. As presiding justice, the Australian president took advantage of the Pakistani judge who was absent due to illness. He cast the Pakistani ballot without the judge's permission (and in a manner contrary to the stand that the absent judge would have taken had he been able to vote). This gave the president two votes and enabled him to have the Court reject the Liberian-Ethiopian petition by one vote.

One can imagine the hostile reaction of African public opinion to such an arbitrary procedure. It was seen as one more example of the successful attempt of white supremacists to retain their precarious authority in a country where they were outnumbered by the blacks 5 to 1. In the end, this imbalance had its effect on the U.N. General Assembly, which then voted by a large majority to terminate South Africa's mandate over South-West Africa. This action resulted in the establishment of a council for South-West Africa to take up the normal administrative supervision of a Trust Territory. It also renamed the Territory Namibia in order to help establish the Territory as an entity entirely separate from South Africa.

As shown by the South-West African debates at the U.N., the United States, like most nations of the world, showed opposition to the apartheid system of South Africa. The ratio of five blacks to one white gives the white government its excuse to adopt measures of steadily increasing severity in order to keep the African majority in a subservient position. What is more, the deterioration of black-white relations seems to have gone far beyond a point of no return, and the South African government is tightly locked into its policy. It cannot relax its restrictions without weakening its authority. It cannot become more repressive without precipitating violence.

When the inevitable showdown comes in South Africa, what will be the situation which the U.S. must anticipate? One thing is certain, the Soviet Union, China and India, no matter what their relations to each other may be, will be on the side of the Africans. On the other hand, unlike its stand on South-West Africa, if the U.S. deliberately continues this present course of financial involvement in the Republic of South Africa, it may remain on the side of the white supremacists. The problem is a vital one for the long-range future of American foreign policy.

One often hears that the apartheid system will eventually be broken down by foreign investment. It is argued that foreign capital would ultimately spill over to the benefit of the Africans. On the other hand, it seems much more likely that high levels of investment will help the whites maintain their control. About all that the spending of foreign capital has ever produced is a large profit for the outside investor himself. The large investors, such as Chase Manhattan Bank, 1st National City Bank of N.Y., General Motors, Ford, IBM, Xerox and other major U.S. corporations, reap profits from the work of Africans.

It may well be that the field of electronics and communications will ultimately prove to be the Achilles heel of the entire South African system. During recent years, the science of electronics gives every assurance that there will be major technological breakthroughs. In fact, within a relatively few years it seems likely that new devices will enable the African population throughout South Africa to be aware of everything that the white man has done, and continues to do, to keep them isolated from their brothers all over the rest of the African continent.

They will then be able to learn what is going on in the rest of the world. The most dangerous situation of all will arise when these Africans realize the extent to which they have been oppressed under the apartheid system while their African brothers have been independent from white rule for many years. The U.S. should take action to immediately initiate a policy of disengagement from white-supremacy governments wherever they exist.

At a recent conference held in Algeria, 76 of the world's non-aligned nations perceived correctly their ability to influence the larger nations in the world if they banded together. In a speech opening the conference, then-President Boumedienne of Algeria was emphatic in stating that the developing nations of Africa would accept nothing short of a new world order in which the rich of the earth would cease to be able to impose their wishes on the poorer nations.

The representatives of the various states were more than confident that the Africans had taken the first steps in this direction and that their combined weight would be enough to influence the policies of the wealthy and the strong. President Boumedienne drew attention to the fact that the so-called "underdeveloped" countries contain "over ½ the world's oil and 2/3rds of most of its other vital resources." With such assets at their disposal, it would be hard to deny that they hold some exceedingly valuable cards—cards which could be withheld to great effect, making the ability of these third-world countries to influence world affairs more than an impossible dream. The U.S. cannot afford to ignore the embarrassing position in which it could find itself if it remains aligned with the white supremacist governments in southern Africa due to the inevitable impact that these third-world countries will have on world affairs.

An additional inflammatory ingredient in the South African situation is the severity of its laws. During recent years, violations have been followed by sentences of outrageous severity, even for the most minor violations. Examples of these violations are:

> Any person who advocates military intervention by the U.N. in Namibia is guilty of a criminal offense punishable by . . . death. [Also, any] African who is found on any premises in possession of a firearm and is unable to prove

> that his act was not calculated or intended to 'encourage feelings of hostility' between whites and Africans is . . . liable to the dealth penalty.

What has happened in South Africa is indicative of how white supremacy permeates all the non-liberated end of the African continent. In Rhodesia, for example, when Welensky was in charge of the Rhodesian Federation, his policies were considered by most observers to be conservative. However, when he was defeated for public office he was succeeded by a line of Prime Ministers, each of whom outdid his predecessor by taking the country further and further to the right. This process ended with the election of Ian Smith who, after long and fruitless discussions with the British over the granting of political and human rights to the Africans, proclaimed Rhodesia's Unilateral Declaration of Independence.

To justify this declaration, the southern Rhodesians attempted to make their position analagous to that stated in the American Declaration of Independence. This was done despite the fact that the American position was completely in conflict with their philosophy of white-minority control. But, the Rhodesians continued to justify their cause by making it appear their situation was similar to that of the Americans. This was clearly evident in the opening paragraph of the Rhodesian Declaration, which stated:

> When in the course of human affairs, history has shown that it may become necessary for a people to resolve the political affiliations which have connected them with another people and to assume among other nations the separate and equal status to which they are entitled . . .

Another effort to liken themselves to the U.S. was seen in the way the Rhodesians made constant references to the Boston

Tea Party. This event symbolized to them, as it did to Africans everywhere, the spirit of defiance to British rule.

Even though the Rhodesians had declared their independence, they were unable to act as a truly independent state. The U.N. acceded to British requests and authorized an economic boycott of Rhodesia. These trading sanctions caused the Rhodesian government to reopen negotiations with the British on the question of future African representation in the Rhodesian government. These negotiations resulted in an agreement which both sides believed would resolve their differences. In order to insure that this was the case, the Pearce Commission was appointed to travel through the Rhodesian countryside to confirm that there would be African support for the agreement. It was hoped that, at least, the Rhodesian-appointed African chiefs and their people could be counted upon to approve the agreement, which provided for the gradual attainment of political rights by the black Africans. The Commission carried out its task conscientiously, only to find that the Africans would have nothing to do with the agreement.

In spite of the failure of the proposed British-Rhodesian agreement, the Rhodesians and their South African allies have continued their attempts to make their repressive policies acceptable in the eyes of the world. A major goal of this attempt has been the policy of trying to persuade the U.S. to grant more than grudging support to their racist regimes by claiming that they are the only "bulwark against communism" and "haven for Christian civilization" in Africa. Fitting in with this argument is the belief of many American businessmen, and of U.S. policy itself, that by supporting South African and Rhodesian economic growth, the U.S. can help both black and white to achieve their goals in these countries. But it is these goals of the white supremacists which are unrealistic. On the one side, their purpose is to enable them to honor the racist policies, and on the other, their purpose is to strengthen their hand against their own special brand of "communism". These constant references to communism are little less than extraordinary when one learns that communism means to the South African:

> Any doctrine or scheme which aims at the encouragement of feelings of hostility between the European and non-European races of the Republic, the consequences of which are calculated to further the achievement of the object of bringing about any social change in the Republic by the threat of unlawful acts or omissions.

Obviously, this definition has nothing to do with the term "communism" as it is understood by the rest of the world. The South Africans' use of the word communism reveals that it is merely another way of giving legal support to apartheid. At the same time, it is an attempt to gain the sympathy of the "free world" in its struggle against communism as interpreted by the rest of the world.

Any realistic analysis of what is actually behind American investment makes it clear that the basic motive is the making of profits. This arises from the benefits which are derived from the low labor costs in South Africa. The view of American investors rests upon the "trickle-down theory," under which some benefits to the Africans will ultimately take place after benefits to the whites have been satisfied.

To be blunt, their theory completely ignores the valid contentions that the blacks do not benefit from this money at all and, even if they did, the point of no return having been passed, it makes the eventual demise of white-minority control unavoidable. A few more pennies trickling down to the blacks from the white South Africans will not be enough to forestall the inevitable. In the long run, it would be most beneficial for South African blacks if American business would seek investments elsewhere—in a country where the benefits of industrial growth would reach the entire society and not just a small privileged minority.

This disengagement of U.S. interest in South Africa is bound to be not only unpopular, but also politically unsatisfactory to the British government. Their economic ties to South Africa are so vital that they have no option other than to justify their position by seeking to keep American business interests on their side.

It was clear, nonetheless, that the position of President Nixon was that the U.S. does not endorse racial policies such as apartheid. At the same time, however, Mr. Nixon stated, "we do not believe that isolating South Africans from the influence of the rest of the world is an effective way of encouraging them to follow a course of moderation [in order] to accommodate change." President Nixon's judgment simply demonstrated a lack of concern regarding South Africa and the benefits which can actually seep down to Africans.

Both Presidents Kennedy and Johnson held views about the importance of the U.N. similar to those of FDR, Truman and Eisenhower. Both presidents believed that the organization provided the most effective way to express their support for decolonization.

President Kennedy made a brilliant attack on colonialism while he was still a Senator. He maintained this attitude during the three years of his presidency. It was during these years that the U.S. delegation to the U.N. was required openly to support resolutions calling for an end to racial discrimination and colonialism in southern Africa. The Kennedy position was an honest reflection of the Roosevelt-Hull advocacy of an end to colonialism.

Unfortunately, the relationship between Adlai Stevenson, the U.S. Representative to the U.N., and Kennedy did not reflect the interplay of personal confidence that had marked the teamwork between President Eisenhower and Ambassador Lodge. This came about because of Kennedy's latent lack of confidence in Stevenson. This was unfortunate because it tended to deprive the U.N. of its erstwhile influence. The importance of the U.N. began to shrink until the organization was almost completely ignored during the initial period of the Nixon administration.

When President Johnson succeeded to the Presidency, following the Kennedy assassination, he continued to give the U.N. major support by appointing Justice Goldberg of the Supreme Court to this prestigious post. Goldberg tried hard to undertake the leadership of the U.S. delegation in New York and only ended his efforts when he felt obliged to resign because of his opposition to President Johnson's conduct of the war in Vietnam.

President Johnson further showed his support for the U.N. by giving the organization full support in its attempts to gain freedom for southern Africa. In fact, he felt so strongly about this issue that he instituted an embargo of all Rhodesian goods by virtue of an executive order. This order set fines of up to $10,000 for companies disregarding his directions. This embargo continued until the early months of the Nixon administration, when Congress passed a law permitting Rhodesian chrome to be imported as a strategic commodity. This was done even though the U.S. was heavily overstocked in chrome. This put the U.S. into a situation of flagrant disregard of our obligations under the U.N. Charter. Except for the Nixon administration, support for decolonization has been a policy to which every President has contributed since the days of FDR and the Atlantic Charter.

In conclusion, it is clear that the Africans are marching to a new drumbeat, and like most of mankind, Americans must march with them. But we cannot do so as long as we continue our present course of encouraging the white-minority governments in South Africa. It is the reversal of such policy that must be followed. The U.S. should make a clean break from anything which connotes racial superiority or apartheid.

The hour is late, but the choice is clear. The time has come to recognize the high purpose which could be injected into American life if we are determined to think big instead of accepting the counsel of those who lack an adventurous spirit. Failure to aim high would force us to accept the risk of sinking into a state of mediocrity. This would be tragic indeed, and totally unnecessary. Far better, for example, to aim high—to encourage a new and more daring approach to our international relations. It would be tragic if we were to reject all aspiration. Without the stimulation of high national purpose, we could eventually wallow in self-satisfying complacency until it was too late to ward off the final decay of our society. This would put an end to any national ambition to create a new enthusiasm for transforming the U.N. into a more influential body for the benefit of all mankind.

The attitude of the Nixon administration toward the U.N. was far short of such dynamism. It was also contrary to that of every other president since the days of F.D. Roosevelt. In short, as we have already related, President Nixon downgraded the work of the U.N. by treating it as only good for the storage of white materials. This is clearly unhelpful to the history of the independence decade, especially if we are now to look forward to the beginning of a new and more cooperative world order. It is pertinent to refer back to Secretary General Waldheim's annual report of 1973 on the state of the world. In this report, the Secretary General perspicaciously asked whether "the member states really wanted an organization which was more than simply conference machinery and a forum for the pursuit of national policies." He observed that "the ability to cooperate in the pursuit of common interests and common goals may well be a matter of human survival." He also stated that if the major powers maintain their present practice of bypassing the U.N., "the revolution toward internationalism and interdependence, which started in 1945, will be reversed and that this reaction will place mankind in jeopardy."

Kingman Brewster and many other observers of the world scene very wisely warn that "political and economic power may run amok unless harnessed by some arrangements bigger than nations." The fear is that if the U.S. does not become the affirmative champion of arrangements adequate to deal with those problems which transcend nations, then the initiative, and especially the appeal to future generations, will fall by default to the champions of centralized world socialism. "It is hard to see how we will . . . stand any chance of competing for the respect of mankind generally if we continue to be more concerned with sovereignty of nations than with the ultimate sovereignty of peoples." This comprises a most challenging approach to what can and must be done if the U.S. is "to take some risks in order to invite others to pool their sovereignty with ours on matters which none of us can control alone."

Such an all-embracing project is not so much out of reach as might be supposed. As matters now stand, the third world represents the largest block of votes in the U.N. and therefore controls its procedures. This control means nothing as long as the great powers avoid the U.N. or block its decisions by their veto in the Security Council, through which all important measures must pass. To achieve this end, the U.S. is the obvious choice to take the lead.

What a magnificent opportunity such leadership presents! If, as may be expected, the President of the U.S. is guided by the same spirit which motivated most of his predecessors, he will have a magnificent opportunity!

There may, of course, be those who will shrink from such a daring project. When one stops to analyze their objections, a new and most encouraging element enters the picture. Is there any doubt that the third world will be other than enthusiastic to find themselves supported in the U.N. by the U.S.?

The long-standing lack of cooperation between the U.S. and the Soviet Union in the U.N. must be overcome. The prospects are not completely discouraging. How would the Soviets react if they found the U.S. in alliance with the third-world nations in the U.N., as they did during the South-West Africa debates of 1959. The progressive U.S. policy during these debates not only forged a strong alliance with the African nations, but also forced the Soviet Union to back a policy which was initiated by the U.S., and to which it was opposed. Inevitably, such an alliance would present them with a dilemma not often faced by the Soviet Union. They would be obliged then, as they were in 1959, to join in support for a more effective U.N., or move to the sidelines, where they would become isolated and impotent. It is not too much to forecast that the Soviets would choose to remain in the U.N. stream, as they had previously, even though this would mean that they were operating completely on the side of the U.S. This cooperation would constitute one of the great breakthroughs for the maintenance of international peace. Then, it could truly be said that the decade of independence which unleashed the energy of the great African continent will go down as one of the great evolutionary events of recorded history. Those days of promise and high purpose will have been truly fulfilled.

Appendix

Memorandum from Mason Sears to the United States Concerning West Africa Following Fact-Finding Mission of 1954

It was very impressive to see the amount of construction which was taking place on every side. Low cost, sanitary housing on a large scale is to be seen in all countries, while everywhere one goes, there is the building of new roads, new schools, new universities and new factories. The atmosphere is charged with progress. Progressive political advancement is also much in evidence—most of all, of course, in British areas. And there seems to be no consciousness of a color line anywhere.

The basic problem so far as I could observe centers around the wide divergence between British and French development policies. Both countries are sincerely and successfully promoting the welfare of the people under their administrations and both aim ultimately to establish political institutions according to trusteeship obligations. The trouble comes because British policy endeavors to develop among the Africans a hard corps of responsible political leaders, while French policy concentrates on assimilating the Africans into the French cultural system and, in a sense, to develop them into the best possible Frenchmen. This is a basic policy difference which gives rise to a number of complications which will sooner or later have to be adjusted. The British, of course, emphasize self-government and from their point of view they would like to see it come as soon as possible. On the other hand, the French, although by no means adverse to the development of self-governing institutions, do not place so much emphasis on it as the British do. This raises the question as to what the political repercussions will be when the Gold Coast and Nigeria become fully independent and by free choice sovereign members of the British Commonwealth while the French areas are still in a dependent status. It is my opinion that the French are very realistic administrators and that if and when it becomes apparent that the British policy is working successfully they will raise their present sights so as to speed progress towards self-government in such a way as to keep political disturbances at a minimum.

So much for general impressions. The remainder of this memorandum will touch briefly on political and economic affairs in the various French and British areas.

French Cameroons. The French High Commissioner, who was out of the country, provided his personal twin-motored airplane and two of the best informed officials so as to permit me to see as much as possible during my short stay in their country. I was accompanied by M. Becquey, Chief of External Affairs, who was also the Special Representative of the French Cameroons in the

Trusteeship Council, and by M. Tirant, Delegate of
the High Commissioner for the North Cameroons.
We travelled from north to south. In the north we
visited the civilized and conservative Muslims as
well as some of the most primitive people that it is
possible to see. In the south we saw pagan and
Christian peoples, the latter being much more
politically active than their neighbors in the north.
Although I visited many of the traditional Muslim
leaders called Lamidos, and was called upon by the
Paramount Tribal Chief in the south who happens
to be President of the Traditional Chiefs
Association, I was unable to observe any
outcropping of nationalism even though it
unquestionably existed. The French, however, did
tell me that they were aware of no desire on their
side of the border for any sort of unification with
the tribes in the British Cameroons.

     British Cameroons. I spent a number
of days in Buea with Brigadier Gibbons, who is the
Chief Administrator of the Trust Territory. While
there I had several talks with Dr. Endeley, leader of
the Cameroon National Congress. In the elections
of last December his party won all of the thirteen
seats allotted to the Southern Cameroons in the
eastern Nigerian House of Assembly. This has
given him a government *without* a minority which
in the end may spell his downfall. At any rate, the
main political fact of life in the Southern
Cameroons is a widespread fear of the Ibo people
who inhabit the Eastern Region of Nigeria. The
Ibos are said to be the most politically aggressive
people in West Africa. They are led by Dr. Azikwe
and are many times more numerous than the people
of the Southern Cameroons. In consequence, the
politicians in the Southern Cameroons feel that if

they join in any way with their neighbors in Nigeria they will lose forever all political identity. On the other hand, the Muslim people of the North are as one with the Northern people in Nigeria. This puts Dr. Endeley in a difficult position. At present he admits that because of the French policy of gradual assimilation into the French way of life, there is no immediate prospect of independence for the French Cameroons. That means that since he cannot, as a nationalist leader, advocate the placing of his people under French control, and since he is unwilling to join the Ibos to the west under Nigerian control, he has no alternative except to let the North go its own way, while he asks the South to remain under British control. His people would thus represent such a small fragmented group as to raise the question of whether he can get the necessary backing from any source to accomplish such a limited purpose.

On the other hand, Brigadier Gibbons intimated that before the next elections, two years from now, it was not impossible that a minority might develop in the Southern Cameroons which could lead to the ultimate association of the entire Cameroons as a federated part of a new and independent Nigeria.

Nigeria. This huge country of some 35,000,000 people is the largest remaining British colony in the world. Population-wise, it is about as large as Egypt and the Union of South Africa combined. It is divided into three regions, the Northern Region, the Western Region, and the Eastern Region. As a result of the recent constitutional conference with the British Colonial Office each of these three regions, if they so desire, may become self-governing within a loose Nigerian federation by 1956 or shortly thereafter. This would make Nigeria a sovereign nation, and a nation which would presumably choose to become a member of the British Commonwealth. On the other hand, as I understand it, the British do not wish Nigeria to be divided into fragments and do not propose, therefore, to permit the creation of a sovereign state until such time as all three regions agree to it. This means that if the Northern Region, which is composed largely of Muslims and is very conservative, does not choose to end their association with Great Britain, the Eastern and Western Regions will become self-governing areas within Nigeria, but not sovereign.

I had the pleasure of visiting the Emir of Kano and asked him how he felt about self-government for the Northern Region. In reply he emphasized the word "ripen". He would not commit himself beyond the statement that his people needed time to "ripen". I was told that he is a very strict and conservative Muslim and is a disciplinarian in his administration.

I also had an opportunity to talk with Dr. Awolowo, who is the Chief Minister for the Western Region. I asked him what his attitude would be in the event that the Northern Region balked at self-government by 1956 and thus delayed independence for Nigeria as a whole. His answer was that he would seriously consider the question of "secession".

I did not have the privilege of meeting Dr. Azikwe, who is the Chief Minister of the Eastern Region, but I understand that he is the most ambitious political leader of them all and is the chief advocate of a Nigerian federation over which he would like to become the first Prime

Minister. The Governor of Nigeria, Sir John Macpherson, was kind enough to discuss with me on a number of occasions the political progress which was taking place in Nigeria. He emphasized that it was impossible to predict what would develop within the next two or three years. He used the term "fluid" to describe the situation.

French Togoland. I stayed for a number of days in Lomé with M. Pechoux, the Commissioner of the Trust Territory of French Togoland. I got the reaction that he ran what the navy would call a "taut ship". There is, however, no question about his expectation that the Trust Territory will be self-governing one day, although he did not seem to feel that there was any particular hurry involved. The most interesting thing he told me was that they had recently discovered very extensive phosphate deposits in the Territory and that this would have revolutionary economic results. On the political side he told me that the nationalist leader, Mr. Olympio, had lost much ground and was no longer of any real influence. The French Commissioner appeared to me to be a very competent but conservative administrator who was determined to do his best to provide for the development and the welfare of the people under his charge.

Because I expressed an interest in seeing as much of the native customs and way of life as possible, the French administrators were good enough to take me to call on the chiefs of a number of fairly large towns. In every case these traditional chiefs showed us the greatest hospitality and all kinds of honors, including exhibitions of dancing and drumming and gun powder salutes. To a man they spoke of a desire to be left alone so that they might develop peacefully under the present French administrators. Every one of them expressed annoyance over the fact that during their lifetime they had gone through four or five changes in foreign administration. They told me they now wished a period of calm. Although the nationalists in French Togoland bombarded the American Consul at Accra in the Gold Coast with requests for an interview before I left British territory—on the grounds that they would not be allowed to speak with me on French soil—I could detect no effort (although an effort was certainly being made) on the part of the French to restrain any political leaders from having an interview with me if they so desired.

British Togoland. Under the new Gold Coast constitution, on June 15, there will be an election in the Trust Territory of British Togoland, as well as in the Gold Coast, to select representatives to the new Legislative Assembly. The issue in Togoland will be whether or not to vote for candidates who favor joining the Gold Coast and ultimately becoming independent along with that country, or uniting themselves with French Togoland even though this would entail a further period of remaining under trusteeship administration. The political parties involved are the C.P.P. (Convention Peoples Party) under the leadership of Prime Minister Nkrumah of the Gold Coast, and Mr. Antor who heads the Togoland Congress Party which favors unification of the two Togolands. Delegations from both parties came to see me to explain their position. To each I replied that the United States was only one of 60 nations in the United Nations and that our principal interest was that all people at the appropriate time—the time best suited to their interests—should have an opportunity to assert their ideas regarding self-determination. The only thing I emphasized was that American public opinion trusted that all campaigning would be conducted by the various leaders on an honest basis. In this connection I received a very poor impression of Mr. Antor. He made definite assertions which I know personally to be untrue and I am quite certain that political morality is a subject which holds for him no interest whatsoever. I should judge that with him, as in the case of other less prominent nationalist leaders, the motivating force was a desire to be a large frog in a small pond rather than no frog at all. The people in the northern part of British Togoland will, of course, vote to a man to be joined with their families and neighbors across the Gold Coast border. This means that there is every likelihood that not more than one or two seats in British Togoland will be held by representatives who oppose joining with the Gold Coast. In the meantime, the issue of Ewe unification has receded into the background in view of the mechanical and political impossibility of devising a formula that could unite those people which are spread over southern areas of the Gold Coast as well as across both French and British Togolands.

The Gold Coast. Under the new constitution which was published during my stay in the Gold Coast, the new cabinet is to be made up entirely of African ministers. The only vestige of British authority to remain will be in the reserve powers of the Governor. Inasmuch as these reserve powers which involve the right to intervene only in such matters as security and external affairs and have seldom if ever been used, the Gold Coast, for all intents and purposes, is now self-governing.

I had a long interview with Prime Minister Nkrumah and, as I understand it from him—and this, of course, can be checked against appropriate documents—the Gold Coast Legislature can at any time from now on declare itself independent and apply for membership within the British Commonwealth. On this point Dr. Nkrumah expressed some concern about the position of Dr. Malan, the Prime Minister of South Africa. It appears that Dr. Malan has recently issued a statement to the effect that he would endeavor to block the admission of the Gold Coast into the British Commonwealth. Prime Minister Nkrumah informed me that he had not come to a conclusion on how to handle this situation, but he intimated that he thought the question was one which should be determined between the Gold Coast and the British Government directly, and not between the Gold Coast and the various members of the Commonwealth. I found Dr. Nkrumah to be a very friendly and a very earnest, and a very astute man. He has spent fifteen years in the United States, five of which were during World War II, so he is well acquainted with the attitude and capacity of the American people. I also believe he is fully appreciative of the tremendous responsibility which lies on him to introduce and lead his people successfully in their first stages of independence.

It seems to me that the British deserve the greatest credit for the way they are cooperating and assisting the Government and the people of the Gold Coast to assume the responsibilities of nationhood.

CONCLUSION. West Africa is an extraordinary area of contrasts between very backward people and very progressive people, as well as between conservative Muslims in the interior and progressive tribes along the coast. Involved also are the complications arising out of the absence of a common language. There are literally hundreds of different tongues. As far as I could make out, the principal mediums of intercourse are Pidgin English, and French, and the Hausa language of the North. It is, however, a very thickly populated part of Africa where there are large territories which will almost certainly have sovereign independence within a very few years. It is an area where both British and French administrators are working hard to advance the welfare and happiness of the people. As such, it seems to me to be a part of the world which the United States should do everything it can to encourage, by drawing public attention to the capabilities of its people and its success in adjusting itself to the outside world.

Index

Baroli, Joe, 127
Batwa pigmy tribe, 127
Becquey, M., Chief of External Affairs, 162
Belet Uen, area of, 59-60
Belgian Congo, 9, 25, 40, 42, 112, 135, 142
Belgium and the Belgians, 8-9, 34, 67, 76, 78, 83; colonial policies, 25-28; government of, 39, 113, 124-126; paternalistic attitude of, 112-113, 142; and Ruanda-Urundi, 26, 149; suppression by, 137; trust territories of, 26, 126
Ben Bella, Ahmed, 15
Berber tribe, 14
Berenson, Ian, 48
Berlin Conference of 1885, effects of, 146
Bill of Rights, example of, 83
Black people, political rights of, 93-97, 130, 154
Blantyre, area of, 100
Boer ethnic group in South Africa, 94-95
Bolton, Frances P., 67
Borders, geographic and effects of, 59-60
Boston Tea Party, influence of, 153-154
Botsio, Kodjo, Ghanian Minister of External Affairs, 111
Boumedienne, President of Algeria, 152
Bourgiba, Habib, political leader of Tunisia, 14, 21, 28
Boycotts, effects of, 37, 154
Brazzaville, city of, 27, 142
Brewster, Kingman, 158
"Bride price," custom of, 130
British Cameroons, 25, 92, 149, 163
British Central Africa, 136-137
British East Africa, 19, 21, 32, 35, 119
British Togoland, 25, 37-38, 91, 108, 111, 149, 167-168

British West Africa, 31-33, 138
Brussels Conference, 113
Buea, area of, 163
Buganda: independence for, 21; people of, 102
Bujumbura, city of, 126
Bunche, Ralph, 143
Bur Acaba, area of, 58
Bureaucracy, inertia caused by, 141
Burma, independence of, 31
Burns, Sir Alan, Governor of the Gold Coast, 9, 65
Burundi, area of, 126
Byroade, Assistant Secretary of State, 80-81

- C -

Cairo, Egypt, 61, 63
Cameroons, 8, 29, 34, 122; British, 25, 92, 149, 163; French speaking, 28, 120, 122, 162-164; independence of, 120, 123; National Congress in, 163; North, 163; Southern, 163; Trust Territories, 28, 120
Canada, 36
Cape-to-Cairo road, 47
Capetown, South Africa, 47, 93
Casablanca, Morocco, 13, 106
Casely-Hayford, Mr., 107-108
Catholic Church, activities of, 27, 125
Cattle: raids on by Masai tribe, 44-45; war over, 130-133
Central Africa: British, 136-137; wealth of, 25; white minorities in, 110
Central African Federation, 21
Ceylon, independence of, 31
Chagga tribe, 129
Charter: Atlantic, 83, 157; United Nations, 3, 6-11, 32, 49, 87, 112, 128, 157
Chase Manhattan Bank, 151
China, 151; Nationalist, 9
Chisimaio, area of, 54
Civil disobedience, effects of, 136

173

Index

rebellion in, 23; Mission visit to, 91;
white minorities in, 110
East European countries, 76
Economy, the, importance of, 42, 47,
154-56
Edmunds, P. K., 123
Education and building of schools, 39,
41, 47
Eguizabel, Raphael, 39
Egypt, 18-19, 93, 111, 164
Eisenhower, Dwight D.: administra-
tion of, 2, 4, 70, 74, 86, 93, 105,
123, 156; on colonialism, 79;
elected President, 17; gift to
President Ahidjo, 122; on Indo-
China war, 16; pro-United Nations
position, 5
El Glaoui, 14
El Salvador, 9, 39, 49
Embargo, effects of, 157
Emirs, Muslim chiefs, 28
Emotions, factor of, 22
Endeley, Dr., 163-64
English-speaking people, hatred of,
93-95
Entebbe, city of, 102-103
Ethiopia, 103, 150; border of, 59-60
Europe and Europeans: colonial
interests, 1, 15, 22, 39, 71, 74-76,
100, 110, 116, 135; and communism,
77; post-war, 7; Russians in, 16;
settlers, 32-33, 115; and United
States, 16, 93. See also North
Atlantic Treaty Organization
(NATO)
European Division of the American
State Department, 77, 128-129, 141
Ewe tribe and territory, 37, 107; issue
of unification, 38, 168
Expansionist activities of the Soviet
Union, 6

- F -

Factionalism, tribal, 125
Famine, spectre of, 41

Fer Fer, village of, 59
Feudal society, 42
First National City Bank of New York,
151
Flake, Ambassador, 112
Fletcher-Cook, Mr., 127, 129, 133
Ford Motor Company, 151
Foreign: capital, 151; control, 2
Fourreau, Fort, 28-29
France, 28, 76, 83, 93, 149; African
relationships, 16-17, 28, 30, 86-87,
141; in Algeria, 16, 87-88; Army
Officer Corps of, 13-14, 16; attitude
to community life, 27, 141, 164;
colonial policy, 17, 30-31, 38, 84,
161; culture of, 27, 30, 162; at
Djibouti, 141; government of,
101-102, 110, 116, 120, 141; Indo-
China defeat, 147; non-Muslim
tribes of, 30; territories of, 93, 138,
170
Freedom: appeal of, 115, 141; from
foreign control, 2; guerilla fighters,
148; national, 1
French Cameroons, 25, 28, 120, 122,
162-164
French Congo, 27
French Equatorial Africa, 53, 102, 116,
138, 140
French Guinea, 102
French Somaliland, 61
French Togoland, 25, 37, 107, 149,
165-167
French West Africa, 30, 116, 140

- G -

Galla horsemen, famous, 104
Gao, town of, 101
Garua, Lamido of, 30
Gaspari, Mr., 56
Gbedemah, Finance Minister, 107
General Assembly of the United
Nations, 8, 11, 67-68, 82, 140, 150

Index

Industrial countries, 18, 22
Information services, American, 119; United Nations, 7
Injustice: racial, 85; social, 125
Inspections, on-the-spot, 10
International: collaboration, 2; communism, 71-73; organization, 4; trust territories, 2, 82; trusteeship system, 7, 19, 92
International Business Machine Corporation (IBM), 151
Israel, 93
Istiglal Independence Party, 13-14
Italian Somaliland, 8, 39, 52
Italy, 2, 8, 17; government, 18-19, 52, 59; officials of, 57, 61
Ivory Coast, political activity in, 28

- J -

Jackson, O. D., 67
Jaipal, Rikhi, of India, 39, 44-45, 57-59
Japan, 2, 9, 85, anti-government rioting in, 145
Jefferson, Thomas, 83
Johannesburg, South Africa, 94-95
Johnson, Lyndon B., administration of, 148, 156-157
Juba River, 54-55

- K -

Kabaka of Uganda, 21-22, 102-103
Kaffir wars, 23
Kampala, port city for, 102
Kano: Emir of, 35, 165; walled city of, 35-36
Kasavuba, President, 113
Katanga, province, 113
Kaunda, Kenneth, 22
Kayibanda, Hutu President, 126-127
Kennedy, John F., administration of, 87-89, 156
Kent, Duchess of, 108-109

Kenya, colony and country of, 20-21, 31-32, 43, 45, 50-51, 69, 83, 96, 110-111, 114, 119, 135, 137; Mau Mau uprising in, 76; nationalism in, 113; northern part of, 61; settlers in, 33, 114; universal suffrage granted in, 136; and White highlands, 55
Kenyatta, Jomo, 20-21, 142-143
Kerr, Mr., 51
Kiano, Dr., 136
Kigeri, Mwami, 124
Kikuyu, tribe, 20, 51
King's African Rifles, 1
Kinshasa, the Congo, 25
Koulikoro, river port of, 101

- L -

Labor: manual, 107; riots, 13, 15; strikes over, 37
Labor Party in England, 76, 83
Lagos, capital of Nigeria, 34, 36
Lake Masai, 131
Lake Province, 41, 43
Lake Tanganyika, 46
Lake Victoria, 43, 130
Lamidos, Muslim chiefs, 28-30, 122, 163
Lang, Andrew, 112
Language, common, absense of, 170; Pidgin English, 170; Swahili, 127
Latin America, politics of, 145
Laws, discriminatory, 40
Leadership and officials, 13-14, 28-30, 33-35, 39, 44, 99, 101, 122, 126, 163, 168
League of Nations, 149-150; mandate system of, 7-8, 150
Leopoldville, city of, 25, 27-28, 100, 137, 142
Leper settlement, 46
Liberia, visit to, 122, 150
Liberty, tradition of, 23

Index